GOD'S TRUTH
MADE SIMPLE

GOD'S TRUTH
MADE SIMPLE

Written and Illustrated
by

MRS. PAUL FRIEDERICHSEN

MOODY PRESS

CHICAGO

Printed in the United States of America

FOREWORD

Dear Reader:

This book is a sequel to two other books: *God's Word Made Plain* and *God's Will Made Clear.* The purpose in writing this book is to pass on to you some of the blessings that the Lord has given me from the First Epistle of John, and to exalt the person of the Lord Jesus Christ.

Because many of the basic Bible doctrines have been covered in my former books, and because the topics covered in this book are limited to the First Epistle of John, they do not by any means begin to cover the entire scope of God's truth, and neither do they exhaust all the riches of truth that are manifest in the five short chapters of John's letter. My prayer is that God will make us hunger for more knowledge of Him and His word.

The book is written in topical style, covering every verse, and some verses are used more than once as they fit into the chapter subjects. I have endeavored to explain and simplify, so that the deep truth of God is made easy for even the beginner in Bible study and yet heartwarming to the mature Bible student.

May God stir us to live closer to Him and make Him manifest to others.

Sincerely rejoicing in Him,

Kay Friederichsen

KAY FRIEDERICHSEN
Wheaton, Illinois.

TABLE OF CONTENTS

1

GOD'S TRUTH ABOUT THE SAVIOUR

WHILE THE ENTIRE BIBLE sets forth the glorious character of the Lord God, it is interesting to note how many of His characteristics are revealed in the short book of the First Epistle of John. The beloved apostle had such a deep love for his Lord, that even sixty years after Jesus Christ had returned to glory John still had lost nothing of his persuasion regarding the deity of Christ—that Christ is God.

A seeking soul said, "I can believe in God, but why is it so important to believe that Jesus is God? Why not have

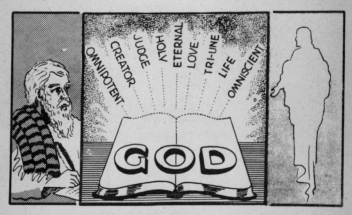

all the great prophets such as Muhammad and Confucius and others who have lived good lives, and have Jesus too? That would make all religions happy." She looked at me hopefully for a favorable answer.

I replied, "The problem with that is that none of these others were able to die for our sins and rise again for our justification!"

How well I remember her face as she lowered her head pensively, and said, "I see what you mean."

Praise God, that lady is a Christian today. But she had to come by the only One Who could say, "I am the way, the truth, and the life, no man cometh unto the Father but by me" (John 14:6).

I. The Lord God Is One Lord, but Reveals Himself As Three Persons

True, the word "trinity" is not found in the Bible, but neither is the word "security" nor "sovereignty" nor many other terms that are used to define Biblical truth. But the teaching of the "three-in-one" God is clearly portrayed in both the Old and the New Testaments, and to each member of the Godhead (the Father, the Son, and the Holy Spirit) is ascribed the same honor, worship, and character which belong to God alone. Each is called God.

Never could the names of beings such as men or angels be joined with the name of God as being on an equality with Him. Yet the names of the Father, the Son, and the Holy Spirit are linked in such a way as to indicate their equality in such passages as Matthew 28:19; II Corinthians 13:14; I Peter 1:2.

Just as *time* includes the past, present and future and *space* includes length, breadth, and height and $1 \times 1 \times 1 = 1$, so in the spiritual realm the Godhead is three Persons, each completely separate, and each fully God, and yet all three are ONE GOD.

To illustrate: Take the chemical formula H_2O. When this formula is liquid, it is water; when it is hot, it becomes steam; when it freezes, it forms ice. All three forms are fully H_2O. One formula, but three forms.

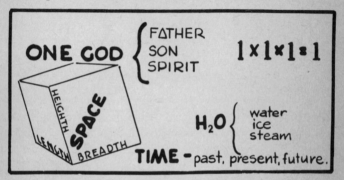

God is one God, but He is three Persons. This is true whether we can understand it or not, for God says so. There are many other things we cannot understand, but that does not mean they are not so. We accept them by faith. We cannot understand infinity: traveling through space and never touching top or bottom! We cannot understand eternity: forever in the past and forever in the future with no beginning and no ending! So also our finite minds cannot grasp the full meaning of the holy Trinity, for this is something that belongs to the unfathomable and infinite mind of God.

However we can do one thing—believe what God says whether our small minds can understand it or not. "Such knowledge is too wonderful for me; it is high, I cannot attain unto it" (Ps. 139:6).

Just think! There are hundreds of parts to the human

eye, and while medical men know how the eye and nerves and brain function to give us the miracle of sight, most of us do not understand it. But we take this miracle for granted every day of our lives and ask no questions. How foolish we would be if we were to shut our eyes and refuse to look because we can't understand it!

We must give God credit for knowing more than we do, and believe what He says "sight unseen." Faith is to believe God is who He says He is and will do what He says He will do. "For my thoughts are not your thoughts, neither are my ways your ways, saith the LORD. For as the heavens are higher than the earth, so are my ways higher than your ways, and my thoughts than your thoughts" (Isa. 55:8-9).

Have you ever watched a baby reaching up with his chubby hands to grab for the moon? Without God, men who are trying to comprehend the things of God with their limited human intelligence are like babies reaching for the moon.

I JOHN 1:3. "And truly our fellowship is with the Father, and with his Son Jesus Christ."

Here John joins the name of the Father and the Son in such a way as to emphasize their being equal. Jesus is called the Son of God, but this has nothing to do with His origin, as having a beginning. He had no beginning. The phrase "Son of God" refers, rather, to Jesus' relationship as the eternal Son to the eternal Father. God could not be the "eternal Father" unless He had an eternal Son. Christ is the "always-Son" and God is the "always-Father."

"For unto us a child is born [Christ, born at Bethlehem], unto us a son is given [Christ was already the Son of God before He came to earth]: . . . and his name shall be called Wonderful, Counsellor, The mighty God, The everlasting Father, the Prince of Peace" (Isa. 9:6). And again, "But thou, Beth-lehem . . . out of thee shall he come forth unto me that is to be ruler in Israel; whose goings forth have been from of old, from everlasting" (Micah 5:2).

When Scripture speaks of Christ as "the only begotten Son" of God, it refers to His being special and unique above human beings or angels, and as being the One Who was begotten of God when He took human form and came to earth (Matt. 1:20; John 1:14), and also when He was raised from the dead (Col. 1:18; Acts 13:33).

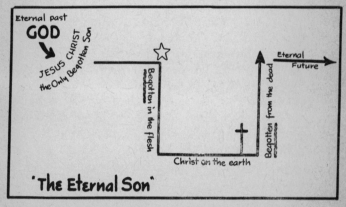

I JOHN 2:22. "Who is a liar but he that denieth that Jesus
    is the Christ? He is antichrist that denieth the Father
    and the Son."

People have said to me, "I believe that Jesus is the Son
of God just as all men are the sons of God." But this is a
twice-false statement. To begin with, all men are not the
sons of God spiritually until they are "born from above"
at conversion. Next, Christ was not born or made the Son
of God; He is self-existent, even as God is self-existent.

To deny that Jesus is the Christ is to deny what God says
about the "Anointed One," the Saviour. "The kings of the
earth set themselves, and the rulers take counsel together,
against the LORD, and against his anointed" (Ps. 2:2).

To deny anything of what God says, is to call Him a liar,
and thus we deny all. In the Bible we have either ALL
TRUTH or nothing.

Here again, John has linked the Father and the Son
together as one. No saved person could deny that Christ
is actually God.

I JOHN 4:15. "Whosoever shall confess that Jesus is the Son
    of God, God dwelleth in him, and he in God."

To confess that Jesus is the Son of God means to admit
and believe and accept Him as our Saviour and our God.
This is what He claims to be.

Suppose that while you are on a trip, your car breaks
down and your child becomes ill. You know no one in
town, so you refer to the yellow pages of the telephone
book, and call a doctor and a mechanic. When the doctor
comes, you do not ask to see his diploma, and neither do
you ask him to fix your car; you accept him for what he
claims to be! Neither do you ask the mechanic to treat your

child; you let him do for you what he claims he can do—fix your car! This is faith.

And this is the way we should treat God. He claims to be willing to save those who believe in His Son. So why not trust Him to do for you what you cannot do for yourself?

II. The Lord God Is Eternal, and Jesus Christ Is Eternal

I JOHN 1:1-2. "That which was from the beginning, . . . the word of life; . . . that eternal life, which was with the Father, and was manifested unto us."

God inspired John to write about his Lord in the same terms as he uses in the Gospel of John: "In the beginning was the Word, and the Word was with God, and the Word was God. The same was in the beginning with God. . . . And the Word was made flesh, and dwelt among us, (and we beheld his glory, the glory as of the only begotten of the Father,) full of grace and truth" (John 1:1-2, 14).

Not only were God and Christ in the beginning of creation but they have always been before all beginnings, aeons without end. Fathom that, if you can!

I JOHN 5:11. "This is the record, that God hath given to us eternal life, and this life is in his Son."

Christ is eternal. He, like the Lord God, has no beginning and no ending. "From everlasting to everlasting, thou art God" (Ps. 90:2). Christ could not give eternal life if He were not Himself eternal!

"Thus saith the LORD the King of Israel, and his redeemer the LORD of hosts; I am the first, and I am the last; and beside me there is no God" (Isa. 44:6). Did you notice who is speaking? The Lord, the King of Israel, and His Redeemer, the Lord of hosts. All through Scripture Jesus Christ is called the Redeemer, so this is God and Christ speaking. But just in case you might have some doubt, listen to the following: "I am Alpha and Omega, the beginning and the ending, saith the Lord, which is, and which was, and which is to come, the Almighty" (Rev. 1:8). This is definitely the Lord God. But now, note the following words spoken by Christ: "Fear not; I am the first and the

last: for I am he that liveth, and was dead; and, behold, I am alive for evermore, Amen; . . . And behold I come quickly; and my reward is with me, to give to every man according as his work shall be. I am Alpha and Omega, the beginning and the end, the first and the last. . . . I Jesus have sent mine angel to testify unto you these things in the churches" (Rev. 1:17*b*-18, 22:13, 16) . Now I ask you, could anything be clearer? Christ is God!

I JOHN 5:20. "And we know that the Son of God is come, and hath given us an understanding, that we may know him that is true, and we are in him that is true, even in his Son Jesus Christ. This is the true God, and eternal life."

Now this is simple ABC English! Christ is the true God and eternal Life.

Perhaps you are wondering why I am putting all this emphasis on Scripture passages that prove that Christ is really God. Well, Christ's deity is one of the most attacked truths in our age today. Many religions are trying to rob our Lord of His deity. They consider Him merely a good man, a great philosopher, a fine humanitarian, a prophet, or a created angel. But if Christ is not very God as He claims to be and as the Scriptures claim Him to be, then God and Jesus, Peter, James, and John are all liars, and we are "of all men most miserable"!

But God cannot lie! Hallelujah! "In hope of eternal life, which God, that cannot lie, promised before the world began" (Titus 1:2) .

God lives in the eternal present He is the omnipresent God who is not limited by time nor space, and He calls Himself the "I AM THAT I AM." No one but He could make such a claim. And yet Jesus made the same claim when He said, "Before Abraham was, I am" (John 8:58) . The Jesus of the New Testament is the JEHOVAH of the Old Testament.

Some have argued that Jesus never did come right out and say He was God. He certainly did! When the Jews kept asking Him who He and His Father were, Jesus replied, "It is my Father that honoureth me; of whom ye say, that he is your God" (John 8:54). For this the Jews tried to kill Him.

When the members of the Sanhedrin asked Him, "Art thou the Son of God?" He said, "You have said it." They turned in fury, crying, "We ourselves have heard of his own mouth" (Luke 22:70-71). In response to Pilate's question, "Art thou the King of the Jews?" Jesus said simply, "You have said it."

However, it is interesting to notice how He replied to the scribes and priests who challenged His authority: "Neither tell I you by what authority I do these things" (Luke 20:8). It was almost as if He were saying, "Why should I bother to tell you? You wouldn't believe me anyway!"

III. The Lord God Is the Creator, and Jesus Christ Is the Creator

I JOHN 1:1-2. "That which was from the beginning, . . . the word of life; . . . that eternal life."

These words show not only that Christ is eternal but that he is the Life. He is the Author of all physical and spiritual life, as well as all material things. "For by him were all things created, that are in heaven, and that are in earth, . . . all things were created by him and for him: And he is before all things, and by him all things consist [are held together]" (Col. 1:16-17). "The faithful and true witness, the beginning of the creation of God" (Rev. 3:14).

This One who began all the creation of God said, "I am

come that they might have life, and that they might have it more abundantly" (John 10:10). The Apostle John says his whole Gospel was written that those who read it "might believe that Jesus is the Christ, the Son of God; and that believing" they "might have life through his name" (John 20:31). Only the Creator could give life and say, "He that believeth on me hath everlasting life" (John 6:47).

I JOHN 5:12. "He that hath the Son hath life: and he that hath not the Son of God hath not life."

It is just as simple as that! One-syllable words! No fear of wrong interpretation here! Either you have received Him, or you have not received him.

But just how do you receive the Saviour? The answer is, "How do you receive a friend into your home?" Invite him in; that's all! The moment you realize that you need the Saviour, and believe that He alone is the Saviour, and ask Him to come into your heart and life, that moment you have eternal life. This is INSTANT SALVATION, if you please! These days we have the convenience of instant coffee, and instant cream, and instant this and that. Well, here is instant salvation! The difference is that many of these commercial products need water added to them. Not so with salvation! We add nothing! We need nothing but the almighty Lord Himself.

INVITE HIM IN! NOW

I JOHN 5:13. "These things have I written unto you that believe on the name of the Son of God; that ye may know that ye have eternal life."

In Jesus the Creator we find all that we need for life here and hereafter; He is the "author and finisher of our faith," the Author of all that exists. He is the very *hub* of the wheel of our existence as believers. The whole universe is held in His nail-scarred hands.

IV. The Lord God Is All-Powerful, and Jesus Christ Is All-Powerful (Omnipotent)

I JOHN 4:4. "Ye are of God, little children [Christians], and have overcome them [Satan's false teachers]: because greater is he that is in you [God], than he that is in the world [Satan]."

In the person of the Holy Spirit God indwells the believer. The Spirit is called God (Acts 5:3-4), and He is called the Spirit of God and the Spirit of Christ (Rom. 8:9); therefore Christ and the Holy Spirit are God.

"Strengthened with might by His *Spirit* in the inner man; that *Christ* may dwell in your hearts by faith; . . . that ye might be filled with all the fulness of *God*" (Eph. 3: 16-19). The almighty, all-powerful God—the triune God!—indwells the saved sinner.

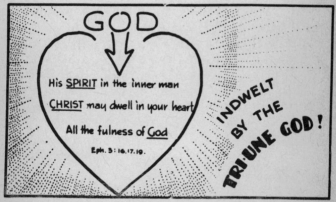

I JOHN 5:5. "Who is he that overcometh the world, but he that believeth that Jesus is the Son of God?"

Just as the only way of salvation from eternal punishment is to receive Christ as our personal Saviour, so the only way of victory over Satan's temptations is by trusting Christ as our Saviour and God. There is surely no excuse for defeat when we have the triune God on our side and indwelling us! Then, why are there so many defeated Christians?

Once again, we pause on the phrase "the Son of God." Remember, this really means that Christ is *God*. Prove it?

All right, here are some references to look up: Isaiah 7:14; Matthew 1:23; Acts 7:59; Romans 9:5; Colossians 2:9; I Timothy 3:16; Hebrews 1:8-9.

The term "LORD" (Jehovah) which applied to God in the Old Testament is given to Jesus Christ in the New. Peter, in his powerful Pentecost sermon, quoted from the Old Testament regarding Jehovah (Joel 2:31), applying that very scripture to Christ: "Whosoever shall call upon the name of the LORD shall be saved. . . . Therefore let all the house of Israel know assuredly, that God hath made that same Jesus, whom ye have crucified, both Lord and Christ" (Acts 2:21, 36). The same word "Lord" is used in both verses. No wonder that the Jews who had subscribed to the crucifixion of Jesus reacted with such overwhelming repentance! They had murdered God, the Messiah! Peter then went on to show them that the only way for them to be absolved of their crime was to repent and then be baptized in the name of the very One they had rejected. This they did, and thousands were converted that day. (See Acts 2:38, 41.)

This is still the only way to absolve Jews or Romans or anyone else from the sin of rejecting the Son of God: to repent, and confess you are a sinner, and receive Him as Saviour. After belief there should be public confession of that salvation by word of mouth (Rom. 10:9-10) and by water baptism. No church or body of men can absolve anyone of any sin. This is the prerogative of Christ, the One whose blood "cleanseth us from all sin."

The ordinance of water baptism is not required of sinners in order that God may forgive their sins. The believer who observes this ordinance testifies that he knows his sins *are* forgiven and that he identifies himself with Christ, that he now belongs to Christ and wants to follow Him.

Suppose you said to your child, "Wear your galoshes today, for it's snowing." This would not mean that wearing galoshes would make it snow, but that they were to be worn *because* it was snowing. So the Jews were baptized because they had repented and had received forgiveness of sins.

Jesus Christ actually called Himself God when He turned to the devil during His temptation, and said, "Thou shalt not tempt the Lord thy God" (Matt. 4:7). Of course God is not the personal God of Satan, but He is supreme God over all things and all people and all angels, even the devil. God is the all-powerful One.

V. The Lord God Is All-Knowing, and Jesus Christ Is All-Knowing (Omniscient)

I JOHN 3:20. "God is greater than our hearts, and knoweth all things."

Omniscience is another attribute which God alone possesses. He knows the end from the beginning, and says, "I am God, and there is none else! I am God and there is

none like me, declaring the end from the beginning, and from ancient times the things that are not yet done, saying, My counsel shall stand, and I will do all my pleasure" (Isa. 46:9-10).

God is never taken by surprise, so when we belong to Him, we do not need to fear the future, for our God *is* the future! What a comfort to know in these days of turmoil that "He goeth before!"

But for those who have not yet received Him, it is a terrifying thing to know that the all-knowing God says, "I know the things that come into your mind, every one of them" (Ezek. 11:5). "Can any man hide himself in secret places that I shall not see him? saith the LORD. Do not I fill heaven and earth" (Jer. 23:24)?

God knows who will turn to Him, and who will not. However, this does not cancel out our responsibility of choice. God fits men for heaven, but rejecters of God fit themselves for hell; they choose to go there.

A man insisted that he did not need to accept Christ as his Saviour, for God knew who would be saved, so if he was going to be saved, he would be saved. So why bother to do anything about it? In the conversation that followed, he was telling me about his business, and how he was hoping to make a big deal the next day. I asked him, "Do you believe that God knows how your deal will come out?"

"Sure. He knows everything." He was very certain that God knows everything.

"Then why bother to go out and make the deal? Why not just stay in bed tomorrow? If the deal is to be made, it will be made. So why bother to do anything about it?"

He rose to the bait. "Oh, no! I have to go and sell." Then he stopped, and his face became red! Finally he grinned and said, "I get the point!"

That man is a Christian now, and rejoicing that he chose to accept Christ. Yet he knows that God had already chosen him in Christ "before the foundation of the world" (Eph. 1:4).

Yes, Jesus Christ knows all things, including the very thoughts of men. (See John 1:48; 2:24-25.)

VI. The Lord God Is Holy, and Jesus Christ Is Holy (Light, Righteousness)

I JOHN 1:5. "God is light, and in him is no darkness at all."

In contrast to the pagan gods worshiped by the Greeks and Romans, John now presents the living, holy God of knowledge and love. The holiness of God is the paramount truth of the entire Bible. "Yes, surely God will not do wickedly, neither will the Almighty pervert judgment" (Job 34:12).

Light stands for truth, sincerity, wisdom, purity, perfection, and complete openness without any deceit. This is the character of God. What a contrast to heathen gods which sinful human minds have invented—gods that mirror

their own depraved natures and limitations! "The idols of
the heathen are silver and gold, the work of men's hands.
They have mouths, but they speak not; eyes have they,
but they see not; They have ears, but they hear not; neither
is there any breath in their mouths. They that make them
are like unto them: so is everyone that trusteth in them"
(Ps. 135:15-18).

God is the "Father of lights, with whom is no variable-
ness, neither shadow of turning" (James 1:17). In Him is
no darkness at all—not even a shadow! In contrast to godly
men of old who met God by visions or revelations, and who
fell down before Him in deep conviction as they saw their
own sin, modern-day people often make sport of spiritual
things because of their impoverished conception of the
holiness of God. They try to bring God down to man's level
as a "good buddy," or as the "man upstairs," and it is popu-
lar to say glibly, "The good Lord be with you!" Sad to say,
the good Lord is not with those who have not accepted Him
as their personal Saviour. God will not look favorably upon
such. "Thou art of purer eyes than to behold evil, and
canst not look on iniquity" (Hab. 1:13). "The face of the
Lord is against them that do evil" (I Pet. 3:12).

I JOHN 1:7. "If we walk in the light, as he is in the light, we
have fellowship one with another, and the blood of
Jesus Christ his Son cleanseth us from all sin."

All praise to God, He has given light to the world. "The
people which sat in darkness saw great light; and to them
which sat in the region and shadow of death light is sprung
up" (Matt. 4:16). This light is our wonderful Lord Jesus
Himself—the Light of the World, the Bright and Morning
Star!

But sinners, the spiritually lost, are like night crawlers,
bats, moles, and other creatures of darkness who shrink from

The people which sat in darkness have seen GREAT LIGHT

light and turn from it. Jesus said to Nicodemus, "This is the condemnation, that light is come into the world, and men loved darkness rather than light, because their deeds were evil. For every one that doeth evil hateth the light, neither cometh to the light, lest his deeds should be reproved" (John 3:19-20).

The Apostle John wrote in the first chapter of his Gospel this testimony concerning Christ and how He was rejected. "In him was life; and the life was the light of men. And the light shineth in darkness; and the darkness comprehended it not. . . . That was the true Light, which lighteth every man that cometh into the world. He was in the world, and the world was made by him, and the world knew him not. He came unto his own [the things that He had made], and his own [His own race, Israel] received him not."

People cannot be saved without personally receiving Christ. "But as many as received him, to them gave he power to become the sons of God" (John 1:11-12).

Dear reader, have you accepted Christ as your Light and Saviour? Are you still among those who know Him not and sit in darkness? Is that what you really want? God forbid! Why not pray and receive Him into your life right now?

Oh, to think of the grace of God, that He would condescend to such sinful mortals as we! "For thus saith the high and lofty One that inhabiteth eternity, whose name is Holy; I dwell in the high and holy place." This should be enough to give the most self-righteous a sin-complex! But, wait a moment. We did not finish the verse. "I dwell in the high and holy place, *with him also that is of a contrite and humble spirit,* to revive the spirit of the humble, and to revive the heart of the contrite ones" (Isa. 57:15). Imagine that! Amazing grace!

I JOHN 2:29. "Ye know that he is righteous."

We sinful beings can never fully understand just what true righteousness is; our minds are so limited and our morals so perverted. But we believe what God says about Himself, and here He says that Jesus Christ is righteous.

I JOHN 3:3, 5. "He is pure . . . in him is no sin."

Christ is the holy, pure, righteous, and sinless One. He "did no sin, neither was guile found in his mouth" (I Peter 2:22). This perfect Son of God was willing to take our sin penalty that we might be made righteous. He is the One "who his own self bare our sins in his own body on the tree, that we, . . . should live unto righteousness" (I Peter 2:24). God made Christ, Who had no sin, to become the Sin-bearer so that we who receive Him might have the righteousness of God imputed to us and imparted to us. "For he hath made him to be sin for us, who knew no sin; that we might be made the righteousness of God in him" (II Cor. 5:21).

What presumption it is for guilty sinners to think they can enter the presence of God even though they have rejected the Son of God! It is not necessary to spit in His face to reject Him. Just to neglect Him is to reject Him. "How shall we escape, if we neglect so great salvation" (Heb. 2:3)?

I JOHN 2:1. "We have an advocate with the Father, Jesus Christ the righteous."

When Jesus Christ came down from heaven to dwell on earth, He made Himself even lower than the angels. He took human form to become obedient to the Father and to be tempted and tried, to suffer and die on the cross (Phil. 2:5-11). But now He is again back in His rightful place in glory as the center of worship and praise of all heaven (Rev. 4:11; 5:6-14; 7:10, 12). If He is not God, then heaven is full of idolators, for they are all worshiping Him!

This same Lord Jesus is today the Intercessor and Advocate and High Priest for those who have received Him as their Saviour. "For there is one God, and one mediator

between God and men, the man Christ Jesus: who gave himself a ransom for all" (I Tim. 2:5-6). Notice here, that there is *one* Mediator —not many. And this Mediator is the *man* Christ Jesus —not woman, not men, not a church—but the God-man Christ Jesus. And why is He alone the Mediator? Because He gave Himself a ransom. No one else could have or would have died for our sins.

VII. The Lord God Is the Saviour, and Jesus Christ Is the Saviour

God said, "I, even I, am the LORD; and beside me there is no saviour" (Isa. 43:11).

I JOHN 1:7. "The blood of Jesus Christ his Son cleanseth us from all sin."

So Jesus Christ is also the Saviour! Therefore Christ is God! Only God could pay the price for the sins of all the saved, and only God could pay the price for all sin, and only God could pay the price for sin for all time!

I JOHN 1:9. "If we confess our sins, he is faithful and just to forgive us our sins, and to cleanse us from all unrighteousness."

The cleansing and forgiveness are only for those who come to the Saviour. Each person must come for himself,

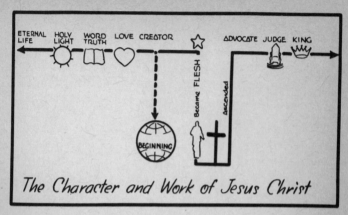

ETERNAL LIFE · HOLY LIGHT · WORD TRUTH · LOVE · CREATOR · Became FLESH · Ascended · BEGINNING · ADVOCATE · JUDGE · KING

The Character and Work of Jesus Christ

and each must come directly to Christ. No one can say words over anyone, or sprinkle water on anyone, to remove sin (original sin or practical sin or any other sin). "Let the wicked forsake his way, and the unrighteous man his thoughts; and let him return unto the Lord, and he will have mercy upon him; and to our God, for he will abundantly pardon" (Isa. 55:7). So it is God who pardons. And yet it is Christ who pardons and forgives sin (Matt. 9:6; Luke 5:21).

Look up the following verses and see how God and Christ are both called the Saviour: Luke 1:46-47; Titus 1:3-4; I Tim. 2:3. If Christ were not God, as He claimed to be, He would be a blasphemer and certainly could not save others, for He himself would be a sinner.

Compare also: I Tim. 4:10 ("God our Saviour . . . God who is the Saviour of all men") with I Peter 1:18-19. We find one of strongest proofs in Acts 20:28, where Paul speaks of "the church of God, which he purchased with his own blood." The Apostle Paul refers to the blood of Christ, shed on Calvary, as the blood of God.

The deity of Christ is truly the keystone of all Christian truth. Our Mediator transfers God's love to us!

VIII. The Lord God Is Love, and Jesus Christ Is Love

I JOHN 3:1. "Behold, what manner of love the Father hath bestowed upon us, that we should be called the sons of God."

I JOHN 3:16. "Hereby perceive we the love of God, because he laid down his life for us."

Did you notice that? It was God Who laid down His life for us! How in the name of reason could anyone deny that Christ is God? And why do some spend their life in aggressive effort to rob Him of His deity? They go from door to door, trying to persuade gullible people concerning their particular beliefs but denying what God has said in His Word. How deluded and benighted is the heart that rejects the truth! Light received, bringeth more light; light rejected, bringeth night!

Two such zealots came to my door, and wanted to come

in. "You may come in," I told them, "if you will listen to
me, and if you yourselves will not talk!" They said they did
not have time!

But then I asked them, "Do you believe that Jesus Christ
is God?" After hemming and hawing for a while, they
said, "No, He is only the Son of God."

"Do you believe that salvation is by faith in Christ
alone?" Again, they had to say, "No, we must keep studying
and witnessing if we are to be accepted by Jehovah."

"Do you believe that you are saved for sure?"

This third question brought another no.

Then I said, "What do you have to offer me or anyone
else? You deny what God says; you deny His Saviour, His
way of salvation, and His keeping power. You are spiritual
thieves and robbers trying to take away that which I do
have!"

One of those visitors is now a Christian. She realized that
she had nothing to offer others, and nothing for herself
either!

I JOHN 4:8b-9. "God is love. In this was manifested the
love of God toward us, because that God sent his only
begotten Son into the world, that we might live through
him. Herein is love, not that we loved God, but that
he loved us, and sent his Son to be the propitiation for
our sins."

Just think of that!

For some hundreds of years during the Dark Ages, the
teaching of the grace of God was almost lost. The Bible
was a closed book. People were trying to save themselves
by penance, pilgrimages, religious deeds, and rites pre-
scribed by the state church.

But the wonder of the message of grace is that God

planned and provided our salvation even before the world
was created and before we were born, and it is even now
available for "whosoever will." It is just as if all the light
of the sun and all the water in the Amazon River were
provided just for one lone daisy!

> Amazing grace! how sweet the sound
> That saved a wretch like me!
> I once was lost, but now am found,
> Was blind, but now I see!
>
> Through many dangers, toils and snares,
> I have already come;
> 'Tis grace that brought me safe thus far,
> And grace will lead me home!
>
> When we've been there ten thousand years,
> Bright shining as the sun;
> We've no less days to sing God's praise
> Than when we've first begun!

I JOHN 4:19. "We love him because he first loved us."
How can we help but love Him?

Someone asked me, "How can I love God? I can't love someone I've never seen!"

There is but one answer: "Then you have not been reading the Word! There God has shown Himself in all His love and mercy and glory, and there you could see Him if you would."

We see God's love in the Bible; we see His love in nature. But we see His love most of all in the work and character of Christ Who is the express image of the invisible God. He said, "He that hath seen me hath seen the Father" (John 14:9)   See also Col. 1:15, II Cor. 4:4-6.

IX. The Lord God Is the Judge, and Jesus Christ Is the Judge

"Shall not the Judge of all the earth do right" (Gen. 18:25)? "The LORD the Judge be judge this day" (Judges 11:27). Here Jehovah is called the Judge. But John tells us that "the Father hath committed all judgment unto the Son: that all men should honour the Son, even as they honour the Father" (John 5:22-23).

Christ was not yet the Judge while He was here on earth,

and He is not yet judging the world. Rather, He is now the Saviour and Advocate. But the time is coming when He will judge unsaved men and women because they have rejected the word of God and the Son of God. He said, "He that rejected me, and receiveth not my words, hath one that judgeth him: the word that I have spoken, the same shall judge him in the last day" (John 12:48). There will be no mercy and grace then!

I JOHN 2:28. "And now, little children, abide in him; that, when he shall appear, we may have confidence, and not be ashamed before him at his coming."

"It is appointed unto men once to die, but after this the judgment" (Heb. 9:27). The judgment of damnation is only for the unsaved when they come before the great white throne of God for rejecting Christ. "Every mouth may be stopped, and all the world may become guilty before God" (Rom. 3:19). They will have no excuse, and will suffer remorse and suffering in the lake of fire for all eternity.

But, on the other hand, believers in Christ are promised that we shall never come before the judgment of damnation. "There is no condemnation to them which are in Christ Jesus" (Rom. 8:1). The only judgment the Christian will face will be in heaven when we come to give account for how we have lived for Christ since we were saved, and to hear His "Well done!" or to suffer loss, depending upon whether we have loved and served Him faithfully. Whatever the outcome, though, we are already with Christ in glory when this judgment takes place. We are safe at "home," and will be with Him forever. (See I Cor. 3:11-15; II Cor. 5:10.) We come before the judgment seat of Christ only for rewards.

I JOHN 4:17. ". . . that we may have boldness in the day of judgment."

Standing before our precious Lord whom we have loved and served to the best of our ability, we will have no fear. Yes, He is the Judge, but He is still our Saviour and Friend! He is with us, and in us, and He stands with us. Hallelujah! Our confidence in that day will be that we belong to Him, and our friendship and sonship will continue right on into eternity!

X. The Lord God Is the King, and Jesus Christ Is the King

The Old Testament speaks of Jehovah as being the king. "For the LORD [Jehovah] most high is terrible; he is a great King over all the earth. . . . Sing praises to God, sing praises: sing praises unto our King, sing praises. For God is the King of all the earth" (Ps. 47:1-7). The New Testament also says that God is King. "Now unto the King eternal, immortal, invisible, the only wise God, be honour and glory for ever and ever. Amen" (I Tim. 1:17).

Now we come to the final proof that Christ is actually God: He is also called the King! "Our Lord Jesus Christ: which in his times shall he shew, who is the blessed and only Potentate, the King of kings, and Lord of lords; who only hath immortality, dwelling in the light which no man can approach unto; whom no man hath seen, nor can see: to whom be honour and power everlasting. Amen" (I Tim. 6:14b-16). (See also Rev. 17:14; 19:16; 21:3-6.)

This is our Lord! He is the invisible God Himself, and it was only when He took physical form that He became visible—as "the angel of the Lord" in Old Testament times, and as the lowly Jesus when He was born of Mary. God the Father and God the Spirit are still invisible. Christ today in glory still has His resurrection body, which is incorruptible flesh and bones, and is visible and tangible. But it is impossible to divorce the three persons of the Godhead from each other, for all three are still one God.

I JOHN 5:21. "Little children, keep yourselves from idols."

Even though John had presented the true God in all His glory, yet he felt it necessary to give this warning.

To allow anyone or anything to take God's rightful place in our lives is idolatry. No, of course we Christians do not keep an idol-shelf in our home where we offer incense and bow before ancestral tablets; Satan has more guile than to tempt us to any such primitive worship as that. He tries to rob Christ of His place as King of our lives! His devices are so insidious and clever that we don't even know what is happening until God's warning awakens us: "Little children, keep yourselves from idols!"

A young wife who accepted Christ after one of my meetings was afraid to tell her family that she had become a Christian. "I'm afraid I'll lose my husband if he knows that I'm converted, for we have always belonged to another religion!" No amount of persuasion and prayer could change her mind. She was content to be what she called a "secret believer."

Not too long afterwards, her husband died suddenly, and went to a sinner's grave. So she did lose him. That dear woman has a broken heart today. Her one cry is, "Oh, why didn't I tell him how to be saved when he was alive?"

But there is even more reason for heartbreak in her life, for she now realizes how she has grieved her Lord. She was ashamed of Him, and chose to keep her family's approval rather than to please Christ.

> Jesus, and shall it ever be,
> A mortal man ashamed of Thee?
> Ashamed of Thee, whom angels praise,
> Whose glories shine through endless days?
>
> Ashamed of Jesus! That dear Friend
> On Whom my hopes of heaven depend?
> No! When I blush, be this my shame,
> That I no more revere His name.
>
> Ashamed of Jesus! Yes, I may,
> When I've no guilt to wash away;
> No tear to wipe, no good to crave,
> No fears to quell, no soul to save!
>
> Till then, nor is my boasting vain,
> Till then I boast a Saviour slain;
> And O, may this my glory be,
> That Christ is not ashamed of me!

QUESTIONS

1. How should we worship God? John 4:20-24.
2. Did the disciples call Christ God? John 20:28.
3. Why not bow before images that represent God? Deut. 4:15-23; Exodus 20:4-5; Isaiah 30:22.
4. In what way is man created in the image of God? Colossians 3:10; Eph. 4:24.
5. How much does God know? Psalm 139.
6. Is God's power limited? Job 42:2.
7. When did God begin to exist? Psalm 90:2.

8. Is God a God of wrath? Psalm 11:4-7; Romans 1:18; II Thessalonians 1:7-9.

9. Does God care when believers are afflicted? Isaiah 63:9.

10. How does God love His own? John 17:23.

2

GOD'S TRUTH ABOUT SIN

IT IS ONLY after viewing the complete holiness of God that we begin to see the sinfulness of sin. Men are too prone to compare themselves with other sinners, and, "measuring themselves by themselves, and comparing themselves among themselves, are not wise" (II Cor. 10:12) . It is as if a man deaf in the right ear would consider himself better than the man deaf in the left ear! Both are deaf!

An accurate comparison can be made only by measuring ourselves against God's demands for holiness. Then our sin is shown to be as filthy and black as it is. Have you ever tried to describe the taste of a banana to some one who had never tasted one? By the time you mix the imaginary fruit flavors that might result in a banana flavor, you have a beautiful fruit salad, but he still does not know how a banana tastes!

The purest thing we can imagine is a snowflake; and yet every flake is formed around a speck of dust. Morally, the purest person we know is a newborn babe; and yet, every babe has a sinful nature. How, then, can we expect to stand before God through our own merits? He will not tolerate sin in any degree in His presence. His very nature abhors sin and all who practice it. David said to God, "Thou hatest all workers of iniquity" (Psa. 5:5) .

In the book of Revelation, John is impressed by his visions of the glory and light of the holy city of God, and

he says, "And the city had no need of the sun, neither of the moon, to shine in it: for the glory of God did lighten it, and the Lamb (Christ) is the light thereof . . . And there shall in no wise enter into it any thing that defileth, neither whatsoever worketh abomination, or maketh a lie" (Rev. 21:23-27).

The very hopelessness of our being unable to meet God's requirements should cause us to see our need of the Saviour.

I. Fellowship with God Unknown by Lost Sinners

I JOHN 3:6. "Whosoever sinneth hath not seen him, neither known him."

Sin is disobedience to God—self-will instead of God's will. Sin is any speck of imperfection; it is missing the mark of God's requirement of holiness; it is failure to glorify God. Sin is failure to obey God's word. All anger, jealousy, impatience, irritability, pride, selfishness, unkindness, untruth, immorality, brutality, and all the other sins that beset the human race and do not show off the unimpeachable character and glory of God, are sin.

Needless to say, we have all sinned. You know it, and I know it, whether we like to admit it or not.

God says we have sinned. "There is not a just man upon the earth, that doeth good and sinneth not" (Eccles. 7:20). "The heart is deceitful above all things, and desperately wicked: who can know it? I the LORD search the heart" (Jer. 17:9-10a). Now God ought to know! The Bible says of Him, "For thou only knowest the hearts of the children of men" (II Chron. 6:30).

The lost sinner has never understood the character of God, and has no contact with Him. He is like a blind man standing in the blazing noonday sun, and arguing, "I see no sun! There is no light!" Not only is the sinner blind to

God's character but he is also blind to the fact of his own sin. He insists that there is no sin in him, and maintains he is not a sinner.

Since the chief end and interest of the man without God is his own will and interests, and his own gain and glory, he reaps the fruit of his selfishness—problems of all kinds. He is hedged in by a thousand fears, and faces eventual damnation. He will find that the devil is a poor pay-master!

A woman whose husband had fallen into the drink habit wanted desperately to show him what his indulgence had done to him, for he refused to admit that he was not master of his vice. One day, while he was in a drunken stupor, she took his photograph. When the photograph was printed and framed, she set it beside their wedding picture. That evening when the husband came home from work sober, he was shocked when he saw the pictures. What a contrast between how he looked a few years before—a clean-faced young man with a smiling bride on his arm and how he looked when he was drunk! As he looked at the unshaven, bloated face of the sot he had become, he determined he would never take another drink. And he never did!

Are we blind to our own sin?

Not only does the unsaved person fail to recognize sin because he is spiritually blinded, but he also fails to recognize true values. He estimates right and wrong according to his own standards, and lowers those standards constantly as he becomes more and more hardened in sin. But God's standards do not change. Sin is disobedience to God no matter what its form or intensity. There is the same round-ness in a little ball as in a big one; both are perfectly round, no matter what their size.

"They shall walk like blind men, because they have sinned again the LORD" (Zeph. 1:17).

The unsaved are not just sinners, nor double-dyed sin-ners; they are threefold sinners! They are sinners by birth, by practice, and by responsible choice.

All men are sinners from birth. "Behold, I was shapen in iniquity; and in sin did my mother conceive me" (Ps. 51:5). Now this does not mean that to conceive and give birth to children is wrong, for God Himself planned that

The Whole World is in the same Boat!

man was to fill the earth with his offspring. But we all receive a sinful nature at birth which we inherit from our sinful parents, who inherited it from their parents, and so on all the way back to Adam.

But we cannot put all the blame on Adam and Eve; we are sinners also by practice. "For all have sinned, and come short of the glory of God" (Rom. 3:23). So this puts us in the same boat with our forefathers, and we had better not try to jump out of the boat, for there is no other boat around!

However, infants and those who are not mentally responsible, although they have original sin and do wrong things, are not accountable sinners. They are not lost sinners. It is not murder or immorality or hate that sends a man to hell, it is the one unpardonable sin of rejecting the Saviour. Babies cannot receive or reject. They are covered by the grace of God until they come to the age of responsibility. It is not said that they are SAVED but rather that they are SAFE. This might be a different age with each person. It is not possible to lump all children together and count them accountable just because they have come to a certain age. Some are responsible years earlier than others. This is why it is so important to have our children attend a sound, Bible-teaching Sunday school where they will learn how to be saved at an early age.

The third way we are sinners is by responsible choice. We are old enough to know and responsible to know; but— and here is a sad fact—men do not want to know! Men are willingly ignorant of God's truth. Like the mule, they have *won't* power!

Willful ignorance is the sad plight of all who have heard about God's way of salvation and refuse to listen to God and receive His offer of salvation. They draw down the shades of their mind and shut out the light.

I JOHN 5:19. "The whole world lieth in wickedness."

Perhaps you are thinking, "Surely you don't really believe that everybody in the world is a sinner!" It does not matter at all what I believe; this is what God says! Instead of being in connection with Him, every lost sinner is "without God and without hope."

On one occasion, I wanted to be sure to get a seat during the rush hour on my way home to Wheaton, so I got to the station early. I saw a car marked "Wheaton" waiting on the track, so I boarded and sat down to read. After a while, I looked at my watch and noticed it was past the scheduled departure time, and yet no one else had entered the car, and so I slipped out to the ticket office to inquire. My train had left ten minutes before! I had been sitting in an extra car that was not connected for that trip to Wheaton!

Imagine my chagrin! You see, I was sincere enough, but just not connected! I was sincerely wrong!

Now, the average unsaved person reacts violently against

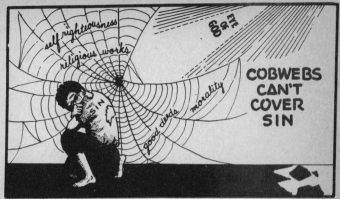

any intimation that he might not be acceptable with God. He thinks he is a wonderful person and making out just fine with God because he is moral and kind and doing the best he can. He might even have been baptized and confirmed and go to church once in a while! But he has not had a vision of the holiness of God, or of God's way of salvation. He is like a person trying to wrap himself up in cobwebs to hide his sin from the eyes of God. But God says of such, "Their webs shall not become garments, neither shall they cover themselves with their works: . . . The way of peace they know not; . . . they have made them crooked paths: whosoever goeth therein shall not know peace. . . . We grope for the wall like the blind, and we grope as if we had no eyes: we stumble at noon day as in the night" (Isa. 59:6-19).

I JOHN 1:6. "If we say that we have fellowship with him [God], and walk in darkness, we lie, and do not the truth."

The lost sinner is not only telling a lie when he says he has contact with God but he is acting a lie as well. Sin is self-delusion. Until our sin has been removed by receiving the Saviour, the sinner is saying one thing and acting another. How can anyone say he is in good standing with God when he has rejected God's Son?

Trying to bury one's head in the sand of "positive thinking" and refusing to admit spiritual danger is "positively wrong thinking!" The sinner's mind and conscience is so warped that he cannot think straight even if he tries. After all, the only way to think straight is to think God's thoughts after Him, and that is to read the Bible and receive the Saviour. *That* is positive thinking!

I JOHN 1:8. "If we say that we have no sin, we deceive ourselves, and the truth is not in us."

We may try to fool our friends and the preacher, and even fool ourselves, but we cannot fool God. He sees right down into every crevice of our mind. "Thus saith the LORD; . . . I know the things that come into your mind, every one of them" (Ezek. 11:5) .

People try different ways to deny sin. Some just make light of it; they consider the drunkard amusing, the foulmouthed smart, the immoral as sophisticated, the violent as brave. Others refuse to believe there is any sin at all, and attribute certain behavior to the weak mind of those who are not able to think positively! Some ignore sin altogether and live as if there were no God and no judgment at all. And there are those who encourage sin, saying, "Enjoy yourself! We're all human! Do what comes naturally!"

The majority of the human race still modify and softpedal sin by calling it by such mild names as "human error," "mistakes," and "slips." But deadly poison is just as deadly under any label. God says, "Woe to the rebellious children, . . . that take counsel, *but not of me;* and that cover with a

covering, *but not of my spirit,* that they may add sin to sin"
(Isa. 30:1). These are those who substitute their own ideas
and remedies which God has not given, and they are just
adding to their sin.

I JOHN 1:10. "If we say that we have not sinned, we make
him a liar, and his word is not in us."

The self-righteous sinner who maintains he is not a sinner is in effect calling God a liar. Now, if God says all have
sinned, and the sinner says he has not; someone made a mistake! Either the sinner is wrong, or God is wrong! Take
your choice! "There is a generation that are pure in their
own eyes, and yet is not washed from their filthiness"
(Prov. 30:12).

Many respectable people in our day have this viewpoint,
and insist that they are "not bad sinners." But to them one
might say, "Then you consider yourself a good sinner!"

Others say, "I'm as good as anyone else!" They are prob-
ably right, too. They are as good as anyone else, and even
better than some, but *all are guilty before God!* One man

in a death cell might say to another, "I'm better than you are; I only killed one man, and you killed two!" But both are awaiting execution. God says of the entire human race, "They are all gone aside, they are all together become filthy: there is none that doeth good, no, not one" (Ps. 14:3). It it a pretty sad picture.

Separation from God blinds the reason, warps the judgment, dulls the conscience, and damns the soul. Jesus said, "If I had not come and spoken unto them, they had not had sin [they were not responsible for rejecting Him]: but now they have no cloak for their sin" (John 15:22).

Some are willing to admit they are sinners but are trying to do religious deeds to make their peace with God; and there are those who believe that keeping the Golden Rule will help their plight, but their efforts to appease God are actually repulsive to Him. "The sacrifice [religious deeds] of the wicked [the unrepentant] is an abomination to the LORD: . . . The way of the wicked is an abomination unto the LORD: . . . The LORD is far from the wicked" (Prov. 15:8-9, 29).

Satan has another trick he uses to keep men from receiv-

ing the Saviour. Deceived by Satan, they try to balance their sins with good deeds, and hope that when they come before God He will tip the scales a little in their favor and all will be well. So if they have been on a drunken spree, they "go on the wagon" for a while; if they have not been regular in church, they go every day during Lent; if they have been cheating in business, they give a donation to the church. And so it goes—balancing, balancing. But as far as God is concerned, no one can do any good at all until he belongs to God. The slate of life must be wiped clean of past sins by the blood of Christ.

It is just as hopeless for a decaying corpse in the cemetery to sit up and announce that he will run for mayor, as for a lost sinner to think he can do anything to please God. You cannot please God until you first have *life!*

II. Fellowship with God Gained by the Repentant Sinner

I JOHN 3:5. "And ye know that he [Christ] was manifested to take away our sins; and in him is no sin."

Here is hope for the hopeless! God is "not willing that any should perish, but that all should come to repentance" (II Peter 3:9). The God of holiness and justice steps in with His abundant grace and love and provides a remedy for the sin problem.

Yes, the death penalty is demanded: "It is appointed unto men once to die, but after this the judgment," and "sin, when it is finished, bringeth forth death." And the "wages of sin is death." BUT—and thank God for this BUT— Christ has given Himself to pay that death penalty for all who accept Him. God's message is not DO but DONE!

Self-help is inadequate. We need Someone greater than ourselves! We have earned our damnation, but Someone else has earned our salvation! We cannot change our way of life or take away our soiled and blotted past. "Can the Ethiopian change his skin, or the leopard his spots? Then may ye also do good, that are accustomed to do evil" (Jer. 13:23).

If it were possible for us to save our souls by works, then why did Christ die? A donation of money cannot redeem our soul, "Their silver and their gold shall not be able to deliver them in the day of the wrath of the Lord" (Ezek. 7:19). "Forasmuch as ye know that ye were not redeemed with corruptible things, as silver and gold, . . . but with the precious blood of Christ" (I Peter 1:18-19).

How sad it is that many are trying to reach God by knocking at the wrong door! They try works, saints, penance, morality, and their church, and yet all the time the Lord Jesus is saying, as He said so long ago, "I am the door: by me if any man enter in, he shall be saved," and "He that . . . climbeth up some other way, the same is a thief and a robber" (John 10:9, 1).

Christ is adequate; He is completely enough!

I JOHN 3:8. "For this purpose the Son of God was manifested, that he might destroy the works of the devil."

The works of the devil are the ravages of sin in the human heart. Christ came to free the repentant sinner from
the clutches of Satan. Christ "gave himself for our sins,
that he might deliver us from this present evil world, according to the will of God and our Father" (Gal. 1:4).
"This present evil world" is the world system under the
rule of Satan. The human race has been captured and en-
slaved, kept in the prison camp of the enemy; and what is
most amazing, they seem quite content to stay there!

But Christ imprisoned Himself in human flesh that He
might liberate us to the glorious liberty of the sons of God,
and buy us back from the slave market of sin.

In my childhood days, as a daughter of missionaries in
China, I often saw tiny little girls with straw bracelets
around their wrists walking the streets, and looking up into
the faces of passersby to see who wanted to buy. The straw
meant that they were for sale as slaves.

Christ has indeed bought us—not to make us slaves and
drudges but sons and heirs! Hallelujah!

I John 1:7. "The blood of Jesus Christ his son cleanseth us from all sin."

The wages of sin is threefold death: physical death, spiritual death, and eternal death. "Death" means separation. Physical death takes place when the body and person are separated; spiritual death is the sinner's separation from God even while yet alive on the earth; eternal death is everlasting separation from God in the lake of fire.

Now, in order for Christ to pay the penalty of sin, He had to experience three kinds of death, and it was for this reason that He took a physical body.

On the cross of Calvary, He died physically; the blood shed was the blood of the King of kings!

He also experienced spiritual death—separation from God the Father. God's holiness forbade His even looking upon His own Son when your sin and mine was laid on Him when He hung on the cross. This horror of carrying the shame of all the sin of all the world was the "cup" that Jesus dreaded so greatly, which caused Him to pray in the garden, "Father, if thou be willing, remove this cup from

me: nevertheless not my will, but thine, be done" (Luke 22:42).

The Son of God was rejected by the Jews, who cried out, "Crucify him! Crucify him!" Now, the Jewish method of execution was stoning to death. But if they desired to add extra shame and degradation to their victim, they could hang the dead body on a tree for all to see. "Cursed is every one that hangeth on a tree" (Gal. 3:13). This was their final insult, and so they were glad for the Roman method of crucifixion to accomplish this sadistic purpose.

Christ was rejected by the Romans, for they used the execution reserved for the worst criminals, and even hung Jesus on the center cross as the most accursed of the three.

But, saddest of all, He was also rejected by God the Father, who turned His face away from Him, so that Christ cried out, "My God, my God, why hast thou forsaken me?" This was indeed spiritual death for the sinless Son of God! And for the eternal, holy Son of God to spend a few hours as the Sin-bearer for the sin of the world, was equivalent to an eternity in hell for a human being! God lives in the eternal present, and as infinite God, hours or aeons are the same to Him. He drank the very dregs of the bitter cup of sin— all for you and for me. He is the all-sufficient Sacrifice, the Lamb of God who takes away the sins of all who receive Him. What a wonderful Saviour is Jesus my Lord! One feels humbled and hushed even to speak of these things.

And yet—let us bow low as we say it—this is the God Who condescended to be our Saviour. He is the *great* atonement for our *great* sin!

Long ago, when the people of Israel were slaves in Egypt, God planned to deliver them from the cruelty of Pharaoh through Moses. He commanded each Hebrew family to select a perfect lamb and prepare it according to His instructions. The blood of the lamb was to be sprinkled on

the two doorposts of the house as well as over the top lintel, as a sign that all who were in the house belonged to God's chosen people. During the night of judgment upon Egypt, the angel of death passed through the land and slew the firstborn son in every house, *except* those with the blood over the door; these were passed over. This is why this feast is still called the "Passover." God said to Israel, "When I see the blood I will pass over you" (Exod. 12:13) .

Why the blood on the door? Is there some magic power in the blood of a lamb? No! The blood of animals can never take away sin or protect from God's judgment. Neither was the blood some sort of fetish to protect the home. Then why?

All the Old Testament incidents and types were part of God's plan to show that the Lamb of God was coming. The message of the Old Testament is "Messiah [Christ] IS COMING!" He has now come, and John the Baptist heralded His advent by announcing, "Behold the Lamb of God, who taketh away the sin of the world" (John 1:29) .

I JOHN 1:9. "If we confess our sins, he is faithful and just to forgive us our sins, and to cleanse us from all un-righteousness."

Just as each Israelite needed to be inside the blood-sprinkled door for safety, so each sinner must personally accept Jesus Christ as his covering and protection from the wrath of almighty God. Our part is to believe on Him, to receive Him; His part is to save.

Someone asks, "But shouldn't a man repent as well as believe?" The answer is, "No man ever truly believed without sincerely repenting!"

Each person himself must believe in order to be saved. No parent can believe for his child, and no minister can believe for his people. Salvation is not a blanket covering for everyone regardless of whether they receive Christ or not. Only those who believe are saved.

Some years ago a serious epidemic was raging in a certain town, and serum was flown in to inoculate the population. Radio and newspapers and telephones notified the area, and everyone heard about the danger and knew about the availability of the serum. Thousands were inoculated, but others were not. And they died. Perhaps they had intended to get an inoculation, but did not get around to it. Maybe some used their favorite remedy from the medicine cabinet, and others tried grandma's "Olde Family Cure," but now they are buried in the local cemetery. The serum was available for all, but only those who accepted it were cured.

What a shame that some harden their hearts when they hear the warning of God! "O LORD, . . . thou hast stricken them, but they have not grieved; thou hast consumed them, but they have refused to receive correction: they have made their faces harder than a rock; they have refused to return" (Jer. 5:3). It is possible to deafen our ears to the convicting voice of the Spirit of God. "He, that being often reproved hardeneth his neck, shall suddenly be destroyed, and that without remedy" (Prov. 29:1).

Neither should sin be recited to God as a sort of ritual to ward off trouble. God only forgives when there is genuine repentance. Remember, He can see the heart. "He that covereth his sins shall not prosper: but whoso confesseth and forsaketh them shall have mercy" (Prov. 28:13).

A dear little old Christian lady came in great conviction after one of our meetings, and told me that she had lied some twenty years before in such a way as to involve her family in a serious situation but that now she was willing to make everything right. What did she do? She wrote a letter to those involved and confessed her sin. After that, her sweet, wrinkled face literally glowed with joy, for her conscience was clear before God and man. Today she has gone to be with the Lord, and how glad I am that she cleared the slate by such confession before she went!

Instead of confessing sin, sometimes men turn in anger against the one who has pointed out the need for righteousness. They may stay away from church because the preacher makes them squirm with conviction. Such men are like those who rejected the truth in Bible days and said to their prophets, "Prophesy not unto us right things, speak unto us smooth things, prophesy deceits" (Isa. 30:10). And the prophets obliged. "The prophets prophesy falsely, . . . and my people love to have it so" (Jer. 5:31).

To be angry with those who preach the truth about sin is as foolish as to be angry with the doctor who tells you

that you have a serious illness! Far better to submit to treatment. "Your sins have withholden good things from you" (Jer. 5:25).

There is no stain so deep but that Christ can cleanse. So instead of trying a do-it-yourself job of sponging off spots of sin by just stopping this bad habit or that, why not come to the only cleansing fountain where all sin is completely washed away?

God is faithful and just to forgive because Christ made complete atonement for our sins. God will never demand double payment. He is faithful to forgive because He has promised to do so. He is just to forgive because Christ paid the penalty of our sins.

A skeptic was making light of Christians, and said, "They will follow anything! Why, I could start a new religion right now and claim to be the Saviour, and some would follow me!"

A listener remarked, "If you would be a savior, then you would have to die for sin and rise again!"

I JOHN 2:2. "And he is the propitiation for our sins: and not for our's only, but also for the sins of the whole world."

The word "propitiate" simply means "to conciliate," "to appease." A guilty world deserved the wrath of a holy God, but the death of Jesus Christ as our Saviour turned away the wrath of God, and the justice of God was satisfied. But we must receive what Christ has done. God only rejects those who reject Him.

When dealing with a young lady one night, she told me, "I am a God-rejected one."

"Why do you think that?" I asked.

"Because I used to go to church and was interested in

religion, but now for many years I have had nothing to do with the church, and I believe God has rejected me."

"It is not a matter of God rejecting you," I continued, "but you are rejecting Him. Will you receive Him right now?" That was the night of decision for her, and she left with the assurance of sins forgiven.

Dear reader, are you a saved sinner? If not, why not pray right now and tell the Lord that you accept Him as your Saviour? Then this will be your date of decision, your salvation day!

> O happy day that fixed my choice
> On Thee, my Saviour and my God!
> Well may this glowing heart rejoice,
> And tell its raptures all abroad!
>
> 'Tis done; the great transaction's done;
> I am my Lord's and He is mine;
> He drew me, and I followed on,
> Glad to confess His voice divine.
>
> Happy day, happy day
> When Jesus washed my sins away!

III. Fellowship with God Continued for the Saved Sinner

I JOHN 2:1. "My little children, these things write I unto you, that ye sin not.

Victory over sin is the purpose of salvation. "His name shall be called JESUS, for he shall save his people from their sins" (Matt. 1:21). Remember now, that the "little children" addressed are God's spiritual children, the saved ones; and His will for us is that we sin "not at all." If Christ can save from hell, He can certainly save us from the love of sin right now. The problem lies with the Christian himself. Do we really want victory? It seems easier to get to heaven by the "skin of our teeth" as it were, and not to mind the godly living!

True, there are no perfect believers here on the earth. Sinless perfection will come when we get to glory and see Him and are like Him, but this is no excuse to throw up our hands and say, "Oh, I'm not perfect yet, so I give up!" God never commands that which is impossible, and He says to us, "Sin not!"

We have no license to lie down and roll in sin just because we still have the sinful tendency to do so, any more than we should go and roll in a mud puddle just because it is possible for us to fall into one! To be saved means that we have been saved from danger to safety, from spiritual sickness to health, from death to life, from Satan to God. All this is put to our account the moment we are converted. Why not claim it all? "Blessed be the God and Father of our Lord Jesus Christ, who hath blessed us with all spiritual blessings in heavenly places in Christ" (Eph. 1:3).

The saved ones in heaven have perfect fellowship with

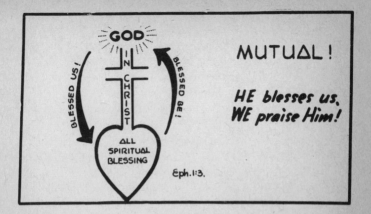

God forever, but even we saved ones here on earth could enjoy continuous fellowship if we would deal with sins as they occur. Sin was cancelled on the cross once for all, but daily sins must be judged and confessed immediately and forsaken. In this way fellowship is maintained.

We do not *have* to sin—not even a little.

If sin is imperative, then just how much should we indulge every day? Just a few lies, or a little bad temper, or a small theft?

God says, "Sin not!"

Perhaps someone asks, "But can't I still be a Christian, even though I am not victorious over sin?"

Yes, for being a Christian is not based upon success, but on having received Christ as your Saviour. But you will limp along through life in spiritual sickness. You will be alive, but mighty sick spiritually! Is this what you want? Well, it's not what God wants!

I JOHN 2:1. "And if any man sin, we have an advocate with the father, Jesus Christ the righteous."

God in His faithfulness has anticipated our imperfection and our failures, and is still making provision to keep us in fellowship. When we do sin—thank God for this gracious provision!—we still have our beloved Saviour as our Mediator and Advocate, interceding for us! We still have contact with God through Him!

Nothing can ever break the connection with God called *salvation,* for this is His gift by grace; but we also have the delicate contact with God called *fellowship,* and any sin at all will sever this. Now our fellowship, which means God's blessing and friendship and approval, is broken, but—all praise to Him!—we still have our salvation!

When the Atlantic cable was being laid at the bottom of the ocean floor, all the equipment was installed and in order, but there was no connection with the other continent. The workmen had to go over the cable inch by inch to find out why the current was not reaching its destination. They found a small nail imbedded in the heavy wire, causing a short circuit. Continent to continent communications had been broken by a small nail. The hindrance had to be removed. The cable was there, but no power was passing through.

In an earthly court, the advocate, or lawyer, can be a friend of the government (the prosecution) or a friend of the criminal (the defense). He is a friend of one or the other. But Christ our Advocate is a friend of both. He is the friend of the government (of heaven) and the friend of the criminal (the sinning saint). But though Christ is our Friend, He has no part in the crime. He is qualified as our Advocate on all points. And He offers His services *free!*

Have you placed your case in His all-powerful hands? Only believers have this Advocate; unbelievers have no representative with God at all. For them, the Lawyer will some day be their Judge, and He will be righteous in damning those who have rejected His atoning sacrifice.

I JOHN 1:7. "But if we walk in the light, as he is in the light, we have fellowship one with another, and the blood of Jesus Christ his Son cleanseth us from all sin."

Here the word "cleanseth" has the meaning of "continues to cleanse." This word refers not to just the one cleansing at salvation but to continued action sufficient for past, present, and future sins. The blood of Jesus can cleanse from *all* sin: any amount of sin, any kind of sin, and for any number of people for all time! Hallelujah!

There is no need for any purgatory after death to purge our sins. God has given the only Purgatory: "He . . . by himself purged our sin" (Heb. 1:3). And we read in Hebrews 9:14 about the sufficiency of the blood of Christ to purge the conscience from dead works to serve the living God. Neither do we need water baptism to wash our sins away, for only the blood of Christ "cleanseth from all sin."

GOD'S PROVISION

FIRST AID

FOR SIN

EVERYDAY LIFE

CHRISTIAN

We not only have the transfusion we need at conversion, but we also have the first-aid kit for every accident thereafter! He gives us life, and is also the Physician to keep us in spiritual health.

Now, a first-aid kit is mighty fine to carry along in your car; it gives a safe feeling to know you have the remedy—just in case. But that does not mean you should drive your car into a telephone post so you can use the kit! So, even though we do have the blood of Christ as our continual remedy for future sin, that does not mean we are going to live a careless life and be presumptuous about our relationship with God.

A young couple who were out of fellowship with God and each other, said to me, "We're not too worried about getting right with God. We know we are saved, and can come back to Him anytime we want to. We don't feel like making up with each other yet!"

Today that couple is divorced. The husband has remarried. The wife has come back to God, but is a heartbroken woman. They found the road back to God was a long hard road after all. No one gets away with sin. Like the prodigal son, the saved sinner out of fellowship with God may have to go by way of the pigpen before he comes to himself!

Fellowship is a partnership in which the same interests and work are shared. Fellowship implies mutual trust and confidence, confessing and forsaking sin moment by moment, and not allowing it to accumulate. Then our blessing is uninterrupted.

Let us not forget, though, that it is a duty as well as a privilege to maintain this fellowship with our Father in heaven. As we maintain this fellowship, sin becomes more and more hateful to us, and the world loses its charm for us. Fellowship is concord of heart with God.

Christian, just what books do you read? What do you listen to and see and enjoy? It's time now to get in practice for eternal holiness!

I JOHN 3:3. "Every man that hath this hope in him [the hope of seeing Christ face to face and being like Him] purifieth himself, even as he is pure."

Never for a moment does this mean that we can wash away our sins or make ourselves pure. All Scripture teaches

against this. But it does mean that we want to be pure, and submit to the cleansing that Christ proffers. First comes pardon, then purity. In time this purity becomes a habit of holiness. The very anticipation of the Lord's return is a purifying hope. The grace of God that bringeth salvation for all men hath appeared, "teaching us that, denying ungodliness and worldly lusts, we should live soberly, righteously, and godly, in this present world; looking for that blessed hope, and the glorious appearing of the great God and our Saviour Jesus Christ; who gave himself for us, that he might redeem us from all iniquity, and purify unto himself a peculiar [special] people, zealous of good works" (Titus 2:11-14). This hope makes for personal holiness, but sin tolerated in the life can dim this hope.

Unless consecration begins at conversion, a life of spiritual sickly-living lies ahead. Christ is not just a "fire escape" from hell. Holiness as well as heaven is the purpose of salvation! We do well to nip sin in the bud each moment of our lives. We are not mere machines; we have been given the choice of good or evil, and we are expected to assert it.

I JOHN 3:9. "Whosoever is born of God doth not commit sin [does not make a practice of sin]."

Through Adam we are born slaves to sin; through ourselves we have sold out to sin; in Christ we are given victory over sin. How then, could we ever wish to continue to practice the kind of living that will not rejoice the heart of our Lord? Adam brought us all into the poorhouse of the debt of sin, and we cooperated right along with him! Jesus Christ reached down and paid our debt and set us free. How impossible that we, who have been bought and paid for and set free, could ever want to go back to the poorhouse and eat potato soup when the banquet hall of God's bounty awaits us!

I JOHN 5:18. "We know that whosoever is born of God sinneth not."

Here again is the same word "sinneth not," which means that we shall not make a practice of the same old sins. Christianity is not a mere code of ethics—of *do* and *don't*—but rather a living relationship with a loving Lord.

A young man brought up in a Christian home said, "I really don't fit in anywhere. I know too much about God to go all the way into the world and sin, and yet I don't want to be a Christian either." Poor chap! If only he would give up to God, and see how glad he would be to belong to God and fit in with Him! "No can can serve two masters." Such a situation is enough to bring on a nervous breakdown!

I JOHN 3:6. "Whosoever abideth in him sinneth not."

This is the key to peace and victory: ABIDE IN HIM! Fellowship with Christ day and night! The trouble is that people want the peace and joy of God and the world and the flesh and the devil all wrapped up in one bundle! This is as impossible as experiencing life and death at the same time!

When a Christian backslides because he thinks the grass is greener over on the devil's side of the fence, he soon finds himself among briars or stones or slough, and he sits down and moans about having such an unhappy life! Instead of feeling sorry for himself he ought to get back where he belongs!

I JOHN 5:16-17. "If a man see his brother sin a sin which is not unto death, he shall ask, and he shall give him life for them that sin not unto death. There is a sin unto death: I do not say that he shall pray for it. . . . there is a sin not unto death."

All unrighteousness is sin, and God does not grade sin when it comes to counting men lost sinners. But in the case of believers, we are doubly responsible that we live a consistent life of obedience and fellowship. Not to do so will bring God's discipline. Discipline is not damnation or punishment: it is chastening or "child training." But it is possible for a child of God to be such a poor testimony that God will have to remove him from the earth in physical death in order to keep him from causing others to stumble. This is called the "sin unto death." The unfaithful Christian may be restored to fellowship, but he will not recover his health, and there is no use to question God regarding it: God has ordained that he will die. His opportunity on earth is over. He is saved, yes; for salvation does not depend upon fellowship—and how glad we should be for that! But he will lose his reward in heaven and will suffer loss for all eternity. (See I Cor. 11:29-32.)

Now, usually we think of a Christian who dies as having gone to his reward. But Christians do not always go to a heavenly reward, even though they go to heaven. However, since we do not know men's hearts, and we do not know who will die because of rebelliousness, we are to pray for all Christians that God will be glorified in their lives either by health or sickness, and we leave the judging to God. This is where the command fits in, "Judge not, that ye be not judged."

So, then, to paraphrase the above verses: If a Christian sees another Christian out of fellowship, and sick because of it, then he is to pray that his fellow believer be forgiven and healed. In answer to such prayer, the Christian may be restored and recover and live longer on earth to be a good testimony *if* God has not already determined that He will take him away in death. This has nothing to do with so-called mortal or venial sin. All sin is sin to God.

How we can rejoice that the "sin unto death" is the exception rather than the rule!

The Christian who is living in fellowship with God may die early in life, but it is because God is saying, "Come home! Your work is done!"

Praise the Lord, we are saved by faith and grace! Faith is

simply the connection between man's helplessness and God's omnipotence!

The cornfield may be full of weeds, but it is still a cornfield! Our passport to heaven is having Christ as our Saviour, but our reward in heaven depends on how we live.

Christian, where do we stand today? Do we really recognize and judge our sin in our own lives? Are we in fellowship with God right now? Come and submit to Him, will you? "It is not in man that walketh to direct his steps. O LORD, correct me" (Jer. 10:23-24). "I acknowledged my sin unto thee, . . . and thou forgavest the iniquity of my sin" (Ps. 32:5).

I JOHN 5:21. "Little children, keep yourselves from idols."

Do we have the idol of rebellion in our lives? If we are not in fellowship, we are literally saying, "God, I don't care about what You say or what You want!" This is idolatry—self-worship. Instead of being victorious, we are defeated Christians.

To carry on in limited surrender and halting fellowship, this is idolatry.

Alas, and did my Saviour bleed, and did my Sovereign die?
Would He devote that sacred head for such a worm as I?

It was for crimes that I had done He died upon the tree;
Amazing pity, grace divine, and love beyond degree!

But tears of grief can ne'er repay the debt of love I owe:
Dear Lord, I give myself today . . . 'tis all that I can do!

At the cross, at the cross, where I first saw the light,
And the burden of my heart rolled away;
It was there by grace I received my sight,
And now I am happy all the day!

QUESTIONS

1. How do we know all men are sinners? Romans 3:9-10, 22-23; Psalm 14; Isaiah 53:6.

2. Who lived on earth and did not sin? I Peter 2:22.

3. What is the result of sin? Romans 3:19; Galatians 3:10; Isaiah 59:1-2.

4. What is repentance? Isaiah 55:7; Psalm 38:18; Luke 18:13.

5. What produces repentance? Romans 2:4; I Thessalonians 1:5-10.

6. What is the way back to God? II Chronicles 7:14.

7. Why does God allow trouble to Christians? Hebrews 12:1-11.

8. What happens to a backslider? Proverbs 14:14.

9. How does a backslider come back to God? Jeremiah 3:13-14, 22; Luke 15:12-22.

10. How are we saved from sin? Romans 3:24-28.

3

GOD'S TRUTH ABOUT THE NEW BIRTH

BOTH THE GOSPEL OF JOHN and this Epistle of John deal with the subject of being "born from above," or the new birth. However, even though this is one of the most important truths, it is surprising how much confusion and misunderstanding surround it. Some think that the new birth means to be baptized; others believe that it refers to reform or turning over a new leaf; and still others suppose that being born again is the resurrection, or even the coming back to earth after death in reincarnation!

But it was to a model citizen and religious teacher in Israel that Jesus said, "Except a man be born again, he cannot see the kingdom of God" (John 3:3). This was no down-and-out wretch, no criminal, but a moral and influential good man, Nicodemus.

The same message has continued on down through the last nineteen hundred years for all mankind including you and me. "Ye must be born again!" To be born again means to be born spiritually, to be converted, to be saved, to become a child of God by faith in Christ Jesus. It is God's way of bringing lost men and women into His spiritual family. So the only way to God is by way of the new birth, and this is the *only* way.

It is not enough to be a seeker, and to investigate religion. "Ye must be born again!" It is not enough to be curious and study the Bible only. "Ye must be born again!" It is not enough to appreciate nature and believe in God. "Ye must be born again!" It is not enough to live a moral life and do the best you can. "Ye must be born again!"

This is something God does for those who come to Him for salvation. It is all of grace—unearned and undeserved.

I. Why Should We Be Born Again?

The most usual reaction to the command to be born anew is, "What is the need for such a thing? I believe all men are the children of God, and God is the Father of us all!"

Pride keeps men from believing God's word, for it is humiliating to have to admit that we are lost sinners and cannot save ourselves and have no part with God at all.

There are amateurs in religion who enjoy speculating about spiritual things, and love a religious debate, and grab on to any new error like trout at the bait. They go from church to church, nibbling a little here and there, and

swallowing error or truth alike, not discerning the difference. They chatter constantly on their views of the Bible. They are religious but lost. They need to be born again.

Another group who bypass God's Word are the moral, industrious, honest, chaste people who have a high standard of life. They are above the average in their morals. But even to them God says, "Ye must be born again!"

Then there is the church-attender—faithful, regular, and unrelenting in rituals and rites; doing, giving, and trying. Yet he has never been born again. Sitting in a church will not make you a child of God any more than sitting in a garage will make you an automobile! However, when you are an automobile, you should be in the garage! And when you are a child of God you should attend church!

Here's another type: the gregarious extrovert who insists that he can worship God in nature when he is playing golf or hunting as well as with the hypocrites in the church. He believes that being grateful for his blessings and enjoying them is all the praise and thanksgiving God needs. He does not know, though, that God has said we cannot worship Him at all unless we are born again.

I JOHN 3:10. "In this the children of God are manifest, and the children of the devil."

God says there are two spiritual families. The difference between the two is very clear-cut. Those who have been born anew are the children of God, and those who have not are the children of the devil. God says, "Ye are all the children of God by faith in Christ Jesus" (Gal. 3:26).

But you cannot become a child of God, you cannot be born from above, unless you believe in Christ. Unbelief is the one sin that damns a soul to hell; this is the "unpardonable sin," the rejection of Christ. Even the moral or religious, unless they trust Christ for salvation, are as lost as the devil himself.

Does this disturb you? Good! For it is not until we are willing to admit that we are lost that we are ready to receive Christ and be born of God.

If you were drowning in icy waters, and I came alongside with a lifeboat, and cried out, "Let me save you!" you wouldn't stop to ask, "Why?" You'd scramble aboard eagerly! But if I rushed up to you as you sat happily in your

garden, and cried, "Let me save you!" you might think I was crazy! Why would you think that? Because you did not know that a poisonous snake was coming through the grass toward you, and so you did not realize your danger.

How the devil fights the message of salvation! He hates to lose one of his children. He is the one who invented the theory of the "fatherhood of God, and the brotherhood of man" just so as to modify the real truth. It is true that God is the Creator and Maker of all men, but He is the spiritual Father only of those who have been born into His family. The day we accept Christ as our personal Saviour, that is our spiritual birthday.

Certainly Jesus and Peter and John and Paul were not all mistaken when they said that unsaved sinners are children of the devil.

Jesus said, "And because I tell you the truth, ye believe me not. . . . why do ye not believe me? He that is of God heareth God's words: ye therefore hear them not, because ye are not of God. . . . Ye are of your father the devil, and the lusts of your father ye will do. . . . he is a liar and the father of it" (John 8:45-47, 44).

These statements brought down the ire of the Jews upon Jesus, and they turned on Him with this accusation, "Say we not well that thou art a Samaritan [half-breed], and hast a devil?"

Jesus replied, "I have not a devil, but I honour my Father, and ye do dishonour me" (John 8:49).

These words remind one of Paul's words against the rejecter who tried to turn men from God's truth, "Thou child of the devil, thou enemy of all righteousness, wilt thou not cease to pervert the right ways of the Lord" (Acts 13:10)?

Self-labeled "intellectuals" argue that all this teaching about sin and the devil is outmoded in our emancipated times, and modern man is too enlightened to believe that all men are lost. That is old-fashioned!

Yes, the truth about sin and hell and the devil is old-fashioned; it is as ancient as the wicked human heart itself! God has not changed, sin has not changed, and the way of salvation has not changed either. "Ye must be born again!"

Unsaved men have worn the cloak of sin for so long that it has become a comfortable and familiar robe. Sin no longer shocks or disturbs them. But old-fashioned truth—that disturbs them!

It is old-fashioned to breathe and eat and sleep, too; and it's old-fashioned to walk and talk and die! No one seems to have discarded eating or sleeping or talking!

"Ye were not redeemed with corruptible things, . . . but with the precious blood of Christ, . . . who verily was fore-ordained before the foundation of the world" (I Peter 1:18-20). How's that for being old-fashioned?

I JOHN 3:1. "Therefore the world knoweth us not, because it knew him not."

What a sad old world! It knows not God. There is much

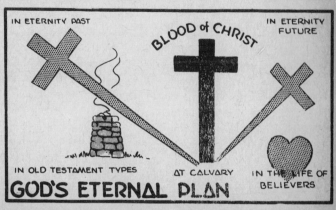

IN ETERNITY PAST

BLOOD of CHRIST

IN ETERNITY FUTURE

IN OLD TESTAMENT TYPES   AT CALVARY   IN THE LIFE OF BELIEVERS

GOD'S ETERNAL PLAN

talk about religion, and much human opinion, but so few
people really know God. Before a man is born again he
cannot understand God's truth, he does not understand
God's salvation, and he often has only pity or scorn for
those who do. The world will not hear the believer because
they will not hear God, and He says, "They will not hearken
unto thee; for they will not hearken unto me" (Ezek. 3:7).
"For which things' sake the wrath of God cometh on the
children of disobedience" (Col. 3:6).

We do not need to teach our children to do wrong. The
tendency to do wrong is already built in.

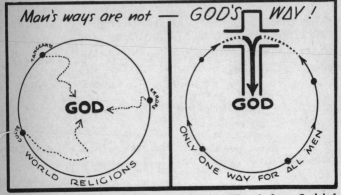

People have sometimes said to me, "This is how I think
it is: all religions are trying to get to the same place, but
they just take different routes. Suppose we make a circle
like this, and all around the circle we place dots representing all religions. In the center of the circle is one big dot
representing God. Now one religion goes around one way,
and another takes another way, and others take yet other
ways, but they all end up in the center eventually! It doesn't
matter how you believe, just as long as you get there!"

The trouble is that no one will get there unless he takes

God's own way. The Apostle Peter said, "Neither is there
salvation in any other: for there is none other name under
heaven given among men, whereby we must be saved"
(Acts 4:12). Jesus Himself said, "There shall be one fold,
and one shepherd" (John 10:16). Jesus also said, "I am
the way, . . . no man cometh unto the Father, but by me"
(John 14:6).

II. God's Way for Being Born Again

I JOHN 2:12. "I write unto you, little children, because your
    sins are forgiven you for his name's sake."

"Little children" is an expression of special endearment.
The Scottish word "bairns" (born ones) brings out the rich
meaning: the beloved born ones of God! This expression
does not refer to babies or little children born of human
parents. All such already belong to God until they come
to the age of accountability. Jesus used a little child as an
illustration of a converted person (Matt. 18:3). He certainly would not have done this if children were lost. This
had nothing to do with baptizing babies or making them
saved. He was simply teaching adults that they needed to
be converted and come in simple faith and humility, as
dependent on Him as a little child is dependent on his
parents. He also said, "Take heed that ye despise not one
of these little ones; for I say unto you, That in heaven their
angels do always behold the face of my Father which is in
heaven" (Matt. 18:10). Now these were not baptized
babies (only adults were baptized by John in the river Jor-
dan), and yet they had a guardian angel assigned to them.
We are told that only the heirs of salvation have angels.
(See Heb. 1:14.)

Notice again, when they brought little children to Jesus
to lay His hands on them, to bless them, and to pray for

THEY BELONG TO HIM!

CHRIST

them, He said, "Suffer little children, and forbid them not, to come unto me: for of such is the kingdom of heaven" (Matt. 19:14). Nowhere in the New Testament is there any indication of blessing for those who do not belong to God. Neither is any authority given to pray for the un- saved (except for their salvation), and yet on this occasion Jesus blessed and prayed for the little ones. He said that they do belong to Him. He did not put them into salvation. They were already safe! He did not baptize them; no rite or ordinance was performed. Christ simply blessed little ones too young to be condemned, responsible sinners.

We too are to come by conversion, in humility and faith. Just as God created man physically out of nothing but dust in the first place, now He creates the believer out of nothing but the dust of failure. This new birth is "from above," and by the power of the Holy Spirit and the Word of God, and nothing physical—no physical agent—has any part in it. "That which is born of the flesh is flesh; and that which is born of the Spirit is spirit" (John 3:6).

Rather than to accept the simplicity of God's way of salvation, unsaved men and women seek salvation in sacraments, and cherish the minutest detail of ritual. Yet God did not prescribe rites and ceremonies as the way to Him. He does not need our help. The new birth is His work in making a dead sinner alive! (See Eph. 2:1.)

We do not become saved when we die, but by being born anew right now! We are born again the moment our sins are forgiven, and our sins are forgiven the moment we receive Christ as our personal Saviour. It is as simple as that!

Amazing as it may seem, all this is "for his name's sake!" In other words, God is delighted to save us, and glad when we come, and His whole purpose is that we might be with Him and love Him as He loves us throughout all eternity. Just think of that!

His nature and His name are glorified when we come for salvation. He has planned that we should be "to the praise of the glory of his grace, wherein he hath made us accepted in the beloved" (Eph. 1:6).

I JOHN 3:1. "Behold, what manner of love the Father hath bestowed upon us, that we should be called the sons of God."

Amazing grace! God has chosen to save and re-create us, and make us His children! Not because we are worthy, or because we are attractive, but just because of His great love. "While we were yet sinners, Christ died for us!" (Rom. 5:8). Oh, the wonder of God's provision! Here is the opportunity for sinners to become God's sons, and for God's enemies to become His friends!

All this takes place the moment we receive Christ as our Saviour. "But as many as received him, to them gave he power to become the sons of God, even to them that believe on his name" (John 1:12). How clear those words are! It is impossible to misinterpret them. This one verse gives the key to all the verses that refer to believing unto salvation. To believe means to receive. It is too easy to think that just because we believe about Christ we shall be saved, but to believe on Christ has a deeper meaning—to personally accept and receive Him. Nothing else, and no one else, can have any part in making us children of God.

"Which were born, not of blood. . . ." Our human parents cannot make us children of God. Just because we have Christian relatives, or church member parents, or a preacher father, does not give us priority with God: each must come for himself. The grace of God does not flow in the blood of our family; we cannot inherit salvation through human blood.

"Nor of the will of the flesh. . . ." Our own efforts and character, and our good deeds and church works cannot make us children of God. All we can do is accept Christ as our Saviour.

"Nor of the will of man. . . ." No minister, priest, missionary, or pastor can make us children of God by praying over us, baptizing us, or saying words over us. No one can sponsor us into the family of God. We must each come to Christ for himself, and God does the saving.

"But of God . . ." God regenerates us when we "receive him" (John 1:12-13).

Jesus says, "Behold, I stand at the door, and knock: if any man hear my voice, and open the door, I will come in to him, and will sup with him, and he with me" (Rev. 3:20). How much clearer does God have to make it? He is knocking this very moment as you read these words; and He is knocking by the good things He has given you, and the unhappy things He has allowed to come to you; He is knocking through your conscience; and He is knocking every time you hear the word of God. Just how long will you disregard the One who knocks at your heart with nail-pierced hands?

He has promised, "I will come in." But we must invite Him to come in. After we invite Him to come in, we must believe God will do what He says, and say, "Thank you!"

He also promises to sup with us and we with Him. Just what does this mean? He comes to stay with us, to fellow-ship with us, and to share with us. Then He invites us to sup with Him and share in all the bounty of His love and

grace. The banquet table fairly overflows with spiritual blessings that make our hearts to rejoice!

To receive Christ is a moment of decision, a date of birth, a spiritual birthday and is the beginning of a life of fellowship with Christ.

I remember a lady coming to seek the Lord one night. She had tears in her eyes, and she said, "You spoke in the meeting tonight about being born again. I have been coming to this church for many years, but I don't know that I have been born again. How can I know this is for me?"

"Do you believe that you are a sinner and need to be saved?" I asked her.

"Oh, yes, I do."

"Do you believe that Jesus Christ alone is the Saviour?"

"Yes, I certainly do!'

"Do you want to be born again?"

"Yes, yes!" Her tears were flowing freely now.

"Then, let's pray right now and tell Him so." Immediately we stepped aside to a quiet corner of the church and prayed together.

Later she said, "Oh, why didn't someone help me to understand before this?"

Too often we take it for granted that people are saved just because they come to church.

I JOHN 5:1. "Whosoever believeth that Jesus is the Christ is born of God."

Believing is the human side of salvation, but the new birth is God's side. We believe that Christ is Who He says He is: Prophet—the Word, to tell forth God's truth to us; Priest—the Sacrifice to atone for our sins, the Saviour; King—the Lord of lords and Kings of kings, God Himself! When we receive Him as *our* God and *our* Saviour and *our* Truth, then we are born of God. "Whosoever shall call upon the name of the Lord shall be saved" (Rom. 10:13).

III. The Results of Being Born Again

I JOHN 3:2. "Beloved, now are we the sons of God."

Right now! We do not have to wait until we die to know if we are saved or not. All the promises of God's assurance of salvation are for us now right here on earth as well as in eternity. When we pray and ask Him to save us, right then He becomes *our* God, and *our* Father. Right after Jesus' resurrection He spoke of God as "my Father, and your Father; and . . . my God, and your God" (John 20:17).

The word "beloved," used here, is a word which indicates God's special love for His children. The unsaved are never called beloved. The family of God is composed of the saved ones in heaven and the saved ones on earth. We read in Ephesians 3:14-15 about "the Father of our Lord Jesus Christ, of whom the whole family in heaven and earth is named."

Now we have the right to come to our Father in prayer and to expect help in temptations and trials. "The Spirit itself beareth witness with our spirit, that we are the chil-

dren of God; and if children, then heirs; heirs of God, and
joint-heirs with Christ" (Rom. 8:16-17).

This is all the work of God. "Not by works of righteousness which we have done, but according to his mercy he
saved us, by the washing of regeneration [being born again],
and the renewing of the Holy Ghost [the making us new];
which he shed on us abundantly through Jesus Christ our
Saviour; that being justified by his grace, we should be
made heirs" (Titus 3:5-7). Did you really take in those
magnificent words? It is not *we* but *He!* How this knocks
out any hint of sacraments or works helping our salvation!
We do not earn an inheritance; we are born to it!

"Having predestinated us unto the adoption of children
by Jesus Christ to himself, according to the good pleasure
of his will" (Eph. 1:5). Here it is again: *His will!* "Who
[God] hath saved us, and called us with an holy calling,
not according to our works, but according to his own purpose and grace, which was given us in Christ Jesus before
the world began" (II Tim. 1:9). Did you hear that? Just
what part did you or I have in that plan? Only to accept
the salvation offered!

Now, since we do not earn our salvation, we cannot hold
onto it by ourselves, and certainly we cannot lose it. God
does not throw anyone out of His family once he has been
born again. "Of his own will begat he us with the word
of truth, that we should be a kind of firstfruits of his creatures [created-new ones]" (James 1:18).

Now hear this: "Blessed be the God and Father of our
Lord Jesus Christ, which according to his abundant mercy
hath begotten us again [and thus we were born again] . . .
to an inheritance incorruptible, and undefiled, and that
fadeth not away, reserved in heaven for you, who are kept
by the power of God through faith unto salvation" (I Peter

1:3-5). Now, if God is keeping our inheritance for us, He is certainly going to keep *us* to collect that inheritance. He will not drop us along the wayside. There will be no uncollected inheritances in glory!

It is impossible to be "unborn" after we have been born again. Just because our children are naughty does not mean that they cease to be our children!

I JOHN 3:9. "Whosoever is born of God doth not commit sin; for his seed remaineth in him: and he cannot sin, because he is born of God."

The "seed" is the new nature given by the indwelling Holy Spirit. We are born again by believing the word of God and receiving the Son of God, the Spirit of God. "Being born again, not of corruptible seed, but of incorruptible, by the word of God, which liveth and abideth forever. . . . But the word of the Lord endureth for ever. And this is the word which by the gospel is preached unto you" (I Peter 1:23, 25).

The words "cannot sin" in the Greek are a present active infinitive in the present tense and mean, "cannot go on sin-

ning." With a new life, a new Lord, a new Father, and a
new home in glory, the saved sinner does not want to keep
on in his old way of life. "Be ye therefore followers of God,
as dear children" (Eph. 5:1). Our behavior should be in
accord with our position; we should act like sons of God!

I JOHN 2:1. "My little children, these things write I unto
    you, that ye sin not."

God has given us the Scriptures in order that we might
be kept from practicing sin. Since the Bible is a microscope
to show up all the microbes of sin in all their wiggly wickedness, we can beware of them.

Reading and obeying the word of God will keep us from
sin, and sin will keep us from God's Word. "Wherewithal
shall a young man cleanse his way? by taking heed there-
to according to thy word . . . Thy word have I hid in mine
heart, that I might not sin against thee" (Ps. 119:9, 11).

Just as it is possible to read and know the Bible from
cover to cover and not be saved, so merely reading the
words of Scripture and knowing what the Bible says will
not keep us from sin. We need to meditate on God's Word,
apply it to our lives, and obey it. God's command to us
is, "Henceforth be no more children, tossed to and fro,
and carried about with every wind of doctrine" (Eph. 4:14).
He wants us to "be blameless, the sons of God, without
rebuke, in the midst of a crooked and perverse nation,"
and to "shine as lights in the world; holding forth the word
of life" (Phil. 2:15-16).

We do not have to be full grown to be normal Christians.
Even a new babe is normal if he is healthy. "As newborn
babes, desire the sincere milk of the word, that ye may grow
thereby" (I Peter 2:2). A healthy babe will be growing and
eating and exercising, and his parents will be delighted.

Christians, is God delighted with your growth? Are you normal children?

I JOHN 5:18. "We know that whosoever is born of God sinneth not."

The beggar who has been lifted to a place of honor in the king's palace, no longer sits in the streets with his broken bowl, begging. The prisoner liberated from bondage does not seek to return to his filthy cell.

How well I know this! After our family had been liberated from the concentration camps in the Philippines, where we had lived on a starvation diet for many months, we did not go back to boiling up a bucket of leaves for dinner! Back home again in America, I remember standing before the abundant shelves in the supermarkets, and fairly trembling with confusion and excitement as I looked at all the foods available. We avoided spinach!

Anyone who still hankers for the old things of sin has never really been liberated from the prison house, and has not yet tasted the good things of the holiness of God.

I John 2:29. "Every one that doeth righteousness is born of God."

No one can do any righteousness at all until he belongs to God. God accepts those who accept Christ, and then they can practice righteousness. Saved people are to be "to the praise of the glory of his grace, wherein he hath made us accepted in the beloved. . . . In whom we have redemption through his blood, the forgiveness of sins, according to the riches of his grace" (Eph. 1:6-7). With such a glorious heritage, how can we help but want to be righteous in our daily practice?

I John 5:4. "For whatsoever is born of God overcometh the world."

Our new nature is born of God, and it is through this that the Holy Spirit gives victory. "For as many as are led by the Spirit of God, they are the sons of God" (Rom. 8:14). As "children of God," we are not to be content just to know we are born-again ones, but we ought to live as full-grown mature sons of God, obedient to God's will.

"Therefore if any man be in Christ, he is a new creature [creation]: old things are passed away; behold, all things are become new. And all things are of God, who hath reconciled us to himself by Jesus Christ" (II Cor. 5:17-18). We don't just "profess" that we are Christians, but we actually "possess" Christ as our Saviour. God warns against those who "profess that they know God; but in works they deny him" (Titus 1:16).

I JOHN 4:4. "Ye are of God, little children."

I JOHN 3:2. "Beloved, now are we the sons of God, and it doth not yet appear what we shall be: but we know that, when he shall appear, we shall be like him; for we shall see him as he is."

Oh, what a glorious day is coming! Some day we shall see our lovely Lord face to face in all His resurrected glory and perfection, but with the nail prints still in His hands and feet. We shall fall down before Him and say, "Unto him that loved us, and washed us from our sins in his own blood, and hath made us kings and priests unto God and his Father; to him be glory and dominion for ever and ever. Amen" (Rev. 1:5-6).

This is the "blessed hope, and the glorious appearing of the great God and our Saviour Jesus Christ" (Titus 2:13). This is Christ's coming again at the end of our Age of Grace, when He shall appear in the clouds in the air with a shout and the trumpet sound. All those who belong to Him shall be caught up to meet Him in the air in a moment, in the twinkling of an eye. This is called "The Rapture."

So now, whether we Christians die or are still living when Christ appears, we shall all meet the Lord in the air, and "so shall we ever be with the Lord"!

But there will have to be a change in our material frame before we can see Him. We will have a resurrection body and—wonders of wonders—we shall be like Him! "I shall be satisfied when I awake in thy likeness." We shall be like Christ with a spiritual resurrection body that can never die; we shall be like Him with a sinless soul; and we shall be like Him with a mind that understands all things!

But in the meantime, we are all in various stages of spiritual growth here on earth. None of us is yet full grown, and we cannot judge other Christians too harshly, since some are yet babes in Christ. The character of a person cannot be judged when he is a baby in the cradle. "Now we see through a glass, darkly; but then face to face: now I know in part; but then shall I know even as also I am known" (I Cor. 13:12). In our human limitation we see Christ reflected in the mirror of the word, and not yet face to face. Now we see Him in words and illustrations, but then face to face! In the Old Testament types and sacrifices, we see Christ as the promised Lamb of God; in the law of Moses, we see His holiness and holy demands. In all these He is the reality of the Old Testament types and sacrifices, the fulfillment of the holy law, the Person in the flesh who will come again and be manifest "as he is"— Conquerer, King, God!

I JOHN 2:28. "And now, little children, abide in him; that, when he shall appear, we may have confidence, and not be ashamed before him at his coming."

When Jesus comes to catch away His saved ones (His saints) at the Rapture, then we shall all appear before Him in glory to give account for how we have lived as His children. We shall come before the judgment seat (the *bema*) of Christ in heaven, to receive rewards or suffer loss according to our faithfulness. (This is not the judgment of dam-

nation of the lost which takes place at the end of time: the Great White Throne Judgment)

On "Rapture Day" when we see our blessed Lord face to face, will we be ashamed, or will we have confidence? All who are saved shall go to be with Christ. That is guaranteed. Our passport to heaven is our membership in God's family. But our boldness and confidence in that day will depend upon whether we have been good children, whether we have been faithful and have continued in fellowship with Him. Anything less than this will cause us to be ashamed and will grieve Him. Just as an obedient child has complete freedom and ease in his father's presence, so those who have been obedient to God will not be ashamed before Christ at His coming.

Once we reach heaven, we will have no opportunity to earn more rewards or win more souls. Our status for all eternity will be according to how we have lived since we were born anew.

A Christian admitted to me that he was a carnal Christian, but seemed not to care too much, for he said he knew he was going to get to heaven. And he added, "That's good enough for me!"

"But that's not good enough for God," I insisted, "for some day you will have to give an accounting for your carnal life."

He was unconcerned. "That's a long way off, and I'm having a good time now!"

"Then don't forget that you will also have to suffer loss even here on earth for flaunting the goodness of God."

He laughed. "Nothing bad has happened to me yet!"

However, since that conversation that man has lost his business, his wife has gone into a hospital with a nervous breakdown, and he has a serious lung ailment from smoking. No, it does not pay to rebel against the known will of God.

Sin will bring trouble. (But that does not mean that trouble is always a sign of sin in the life of a Christian.) "Be sure your sin will find you out!" It will find us out in our body, in our family, in material things, in trouble and sorrow, and—saddest of all—it will find us out when we come face to face with Almighty God. How much better to be "obedient children, not fashioning yourselves according to the former lusts. . . . But as he which hath called you is holy, so be ye holy in all manner of conversation [conduct]" (I Peter 1:14-15). Our new life as a child of God is to make us not only happy but holy!

I John 5:2. "We love the children of God, when we love God."

Another of the sequences of being born again is our love for God and all those who belong to Him. A heart filled with love for God cannot harbor hate for others. What a heartbreak it must be for God to see the quarreling and bickering that is sometimes seen in Christian circles! We know such strife is wrong; the unsaved know it is wrong. So why let it continue? It's time for a housecleaning! "Judgment must begin at the house of God." Children of God, let's make the dust fly! Dig out those dark corners of secret sin, that closet of unconfessed grudges, those old boxes of bad habits! How horrible they must appear to our holy God!

I JOHN 4:7. "Everyone that loveth is born of God, and knoweth God."

To belong to God is to love Him, and to love Him is to love others. We see a chain reaction! God's love to us causes us to love Him, and our love to Him causes us to love others.

I JOHN 3:18. "Little children, let us not love in word, neither in tongue, but in deed and in truth."

The little children of God are to have more than just a "say-so" love; they are to have a "do-so" love as well. Love does not stop by saying kind things and making kind promises; it puts shoes to the promises by caring for the needs of fellow-believers. Love makes life worth living.

Love's worst enemy is self-love. Selfishness is the core of all evil. Self-love robs God of His place on the throne of our lives; it robs others of the love and care they need; and it robs us of the peace and happiness that we so desire. Self is a pretty poor object to love! A person who is all wrapped up in himself is a mighty small bundle!

I JOHN 5:21. "Little children, keep yourselves from idols."

How suitable a challenge this is! It is not enough to be a child of God, He wants us to be good children, and to love and obey Him as well.

My own parents were missionaries under the China Inland Mission for thirty years, and all four of us children were born in China. Our mission stations were far up the Yangtse River, so when it was time for us to start school, we had to go a month's journey downriver to the boarding school. Naturally, it was impossible for us to go home for vacations, so we stayed right there in school year after year. I was fifteen when I saw my mother again!

How embarrassed I was when she hugged and kissed me! I had not been hugged and loved in all those years, and now here was a strange woman kissing and weeping over me! I shrank away.

Her mother heart must have yearned for my love and response, and how hard she tried to win my confidence in the weeks that followed! Her own daughter was a stranger to her!

Can it be that we are treating our heavenly Father thus? He has never failed us; He has never forsaken us! Then why do we so often break His heart by our indifference and disobedience? May He forgive us!

Friend, as you read these words, can it be that you have never yet received Christ as your personal Saviour? Can it be that you have never been born again?

He is speaking to you right now, and saying, "Will you let me come into your heart?"

Have you any room for Jesus,
He Who bore your load of sin?
As He stands and asks admission,
Sinner, will you let Him in?

Room for pleasure, room for business,
But for Christ the Crucified,
Not a place that He can enter,
In the heart for which He died!

Have you any room for Jesus,
As in grace He calls again.
Oh, today is time accepted,
Tomorrow you may call in vain!

Room for Jesus, King of Glory!
Hasten now, His word obey;

Swing the heart's door widely open,
Bid Him enter while you may!

QUESTIONS

1. What is the one condition for entering the kingdom of God or becoming a member of God's family?
2. What is the spiritual condition of those who have not been born again? Ephesians 2:1.
3. Can the unsaved man please God? Romans 8:8.
4. Does not God consider some unsaved people good? Romans 3:12.
5. What does God use in bringing about the salvation of a lost person? I Corinthians 4:15; I Peter 1:23; James 1:18; John 3:5.
6. What does the "water" symbolize in connection with the new birth? John 4:14; 7:37-39; Ephesians 5:26.
7. What part does baptism or any rituals have in the new birth? John 1:13.
8. What is the character of the new nature of the child of God? Ephesians 4:24; Colossians 3:10; Philippians 1:11.

4

GOD'S TRUTH ABOUT LOVE

ONLY THE CHRISTIAN has a God of love. Heathen temples are filled with idols—vicious, fearful imaginary gods that constantly demand appeasement.

One temple I visited as a girl in China had a thousand gods, each more hideous than the other. While I was there, I watched sad-faced devotees enter the gloomy, musty-smelling shrine, drop their cash into the money box, light an incense stick, and fall to their knees and knock their head three times on the floor before each idol. But none of these fearsome, evil-looking lumps of clay were named Mercy or Love.

Our living God of Glory is the God of love and grace. And He must have an object upon which to lavish His love and grace. God's grace is not poured out upon things, nor even upon animals, but He made man in His own image so that He might have someone to love who could love Him in return. Grace is God's love in action!

How wonderful to know that the Almighty God cared enough to create you and me that He might bestow His love upon us and receive love from us! "That in the ages to come he might shew the exceeding riches of his grace in his kindness toward us through Christ Jesus" (Eph. 2:7).

God's love does not wear out with the giving, nor become threadbare with time, and it will not diminish with many recipients. The love of God will meet every human need for time and eternity.

The Lord of glory is indeed wholly love, but He is also wholly and completely holy. He loves all mankind, but He hates sin. He will not overlook or condone sin in any form. Depraved men and women can never fully understand the meaning of the holy love of God because they do not grasp the exceeding sinfulness of sin.

I. How God Has Shown Forth His Love and Grace

I JOHN 3:16. "Hereby perceive we the love of God, because he laid down his life for us."

God is not like sinful human beings who are content to overlook sin in others because they have so much sin of their own. We might say, "I'll forgive you, let's be friends and forget all about our quarrel!" But God cannot do this, for He is holy, and cannot close His eyes to man's sins and pass them over as if they had never been committed.

The only way that the holiness and justice of God could be reconciled with His love was for God Himself to pay the death penalty that we deserved. He could not excuse the sinner until the penalty of sin was paid. So He showed His love by voluntarily paying our debt and giving His life for us. What a way to show love! In John 3:16 as well as in I John 3:16 the same thought has been given: God's love in giving His Son for sinners. "For God so loved the world, that he gave his only begotten Son, that whosoever believeth in him should not perish, but have everlasting life."

I JOHN 3:1. "Behold, what manner of love the Father hath bestowed upon us, that we should be called the sons of God."

Whenever you read the word "behold" it means "Stop! Look! Listen!" The word "behold" in this verse says: Here is something worth looking into! Here is the most amazing thing in the world! The Almighty has chosen to make guilty lost sinners His own children!

If there were no other proof that the Bible is truly inspired of God, this verse would do it; for it portrays an unimaginable kind of love which no man could ever have thought up. "What manner of love," means a special, foreign kind of love which we cannot know apart from God.

Yes, we do know some loves, but none can compare with the love of the holy God for sinful man.

We know the love of sweethearts and husbands and wives: "Cupid love." This is based upon the natural affinity between man and woman. A young man seeking a bride watches for the most attractive girl who will have him. Unfortunately, he sometimes finds out too late that love is blind! The Greek word for this cupid love is *eros*, and is nowhere found in the New Testament. This *eros* love very often is mixed with selfishness even at its best, and there is the desire to be loved and served, and to "have and to hold," instead of genuine concern for the well-being of the one loved. Divorce and broken homes speak only too evidently of such.

After our liberation from the prison camps, we were returning to America on a repatriation ship loaded with civilians and soldiers, and on this ship one whole deck was given over for the mentally ill. The guard told us, "Most of these men are perfectly normal most of the time, but almost every one has a background of unhappy home life. One has a sweetheart who married someone else; another has an unfaithful wife; and others have received 'Dear John' letters asking for divorce. When they read those letters they become violent. Such emotional problems are more responsible for their illness than battle fatigue."

Yes, human love falls far short of the love of God, who says, "I have loved thee with an everlasting love (Jer. 31:3).

The true story of a Christian soldier who came home wounded from battle only to find his fiancée had married

another, goes on to say that that young man sat down and wrote our glorious hymn:

> Loved with everlasting love,
> Led by grace that love to know,
> Spirit, breathing from above,
> Thou hast taught me it is so!
> Oh, this full and perfect peace!
> Oh, this transport all divine!
> In a love which cannot cease,
> I am His, and He is mine!

That young man understood something of the difference between human and divine love.

God does not choose the lovely or the worthy. He came to seek and to save that which was lost; He came to call sinners to repentance. This is GRACE! Grace enough for all our need, whoever we may be, or however sinful we may be!

The Lord is never weary of receiving repentant sinners and forgiving their many sins. "Where sin abounded, grace did much more abound." Throughout history sin has widened its circle of wickedness, but God's love and grace have gone still further. Praise His Name!

This sublime love of God transcends even the love of parents for their children. How beautiful is the love of a mother for a sickly child, or the love of a father for his problem boy! Yet in each case the blood of the parent flows in the veins of the child, and his love is based upon the family tie. It is his own child. But the lost sinner is not the child of God, and has no personal claims upon Him at all. If it were not for the grace of God, the sinner would have nothing and be nothing. "By the grace of God I am what I am."

Even in family love, however, parents sometimes fail their children. Sad it is to see careless mothers and brutish fathers, and homes where children are neglected, coming home from school to vend for themselves while mother is playing cards and father is playing golf, or both are in the tavern.

In heathen lands it is not unusual to see babies left in alleys, thrown into the river, or left to be eaten by wild animals in the bush. In America, infants are left on door-

NEGLECTED!

steps or in railway stations. Yes, a mother may forget her babe, but God says He will never forget us!

Another type of love we know is brotherly love, called in the Greek *philadelphia*. This word stands for the natural liking of people for their friends, countryman for countryman. But human beings can also have the love described by the Greek word *agape*, the word used to describe God's love. For instance, in John 15:13, "Greater love hath no man than this, that a man lay down his life for his friend," the word for love is *agape*. The love described in this verse is the most unselfish kind of love human beings can demonstrate, but it is still far short of Christ's love. No wonder John cries out in worshipful wonder, "Behold, what manner of love!"

Oh, friends, let's wrench ourselves away from just thinking of riches and comforts and pleasures and people and clothes, and look at God's love! Look away from vanity and see reality!

I JOHN 4:9. "In this was manifested [shown forth] the love of God toward us, because that God sent his only begotten Son into the world, that we might live through him."

God is the source of genuine love—unconditional, unsought, and unbought. It is given to us; it is all of GRACE! "That we might live through him" implies that we are lost and dead in sins until we come to Christ. "And you hath he quickened [made alive], who were dead in trespasses and sins: . . . Even when we were dead in sins, [God] hath quickened us together with Christ" (Eph. 2:1, 5).

I JOHN 4:10. "Herein is love, not that we loved God, but that he loved us, and sent his Son to be the propitiation for our sins."

This also implies that the whole world is lost in sin and needs the Saviour to turn away God's wrath. "He that believeth not the Son shall not see life; but the wrath of God abideth on him" (John 3:36). "For the wrath of God is revealed from heaven against all ungodliness and unrighteousness of men" (Rom. 1:18). "Pour out the vials of the wrath of God upon the earth" (Rev. 16:1). "He treadeth the winepress of the fierceness and wrath of Almighty God" (Rev. 19:15). So you see God is not all soft, unqualified kindness; He is also the God of wrath—a wrath revealed against those who neglect Christ.

How anyone can live day after day in utter disregard of the warnings of the Word of God is hard to understand! It is not that they do not know the truth, but "they are willingly ignorant of" what God says, and that will not be a good enough excuse in the day of judgment.

"Not that we loved God" shows that the unsaved do not love God, and yet people insist, "Of course, I love God! What do you think I am, a heathen?"

Why are sinners so indignant when anyone implies that they might not love God? And yet their lives demonstrate that they live merely for comforts and pleasure. "For men shall be lovers of their own selves, . . . lovers of pleasure more than lovers of God" (II Tim. 3:2, 4). "Know ye not that the friendship with the world is enmity with God" (James 4:4)?

I JOHN 4:8. "God is love."

This is the most quoted and yet least understood verse in the Bible. Since love has its origin in God, it is impossible to love aright until we belong to Him. His love, shed abroad in our hearts by the Holy Spirit should flow forth in love to our Christian brothers and sisters and to the unsaved. If we love God, He will occupy a conspicuous place in our thoughts and plans. But human beings can demonstrate also the love described by the Greek word *agape*, the word used in the New Testament to describe God's love. For instance, in John 15:13, "Greater love hath no man than this, that a man lay down his life for his friend," the word for love is *agape*. The love described in this verse is the most unselfish kind of love human beings can demonstrate, but it is still far short of Christ's

love, for He gave His life for His enemies. "While we were yet sinners, Christ died for us."

Agape love is not a shallow liking of people because they appeal to us. The definition of genuine love (God's kind of love) is: Love is the desire for, and the delight in, the well-being of the one loved. Such love has in it no element of selfishness.

The love of God places a value upon the worthless sinner, and then loves him for the very value that He Himself placed upon him! Can you imagine that? And what was the value at which God valued us? It was so great that He gave His Son to die for us and to redeem us.

At the cross we see the love that shrinks at no sacrifice. Such tremendous truth does not affect us, however, unless we think on it. The Apostle John did take time to think about God's love. No wonder he cried out in worshipful wonder, "Behold, what manner of love the Father hath bestowed upon us. . . ."

I JOHN 4:8. "He that loveth not knoweth not God; for God is love."

Now this verse is certainly not speaking of mere human affection. When a boy falls in love with a pretty girl, his love is not the love John is speaking about in these verses.

A man said to me, "Why, I'm as good a Christian as anybody else. The Bible says that God is love, and those who love are born of God. I love my wife and son, so I belong to God!"

Isn't it strange how people can quote Bible verses and get the meaning so mixed up! It would be amusing if it were not so pathetic. Well, I asked that man and his wife if they would read the fourth chapter of the Epistle of John with me. They agreed to, and the Word of God spoke for itself. When we had finished, the man looked up and said quietly, "I guess I misinterpreted somewhat!" Thank God, he and his wife came to know the love of Christ for them, and a new love for each other as well!

II. What Is Our Part in Accepting God's Love?

I JOHN 4:19. "We love him, because he first loved us."

God has made all the advances towards us, and now it is time for us to respond by loving Him. We may grow into the knowledge of His love, and grow into the realization of our need for Him, and grow into understanding that Christ alone is the Saviour, but there the "growing-into" ends! The decision to accept God's love is as instantaneous as the moment of physical birth, for this is spiritual birth.

When you go to the store, and see the item you need, and want what you see, then you make your decision to buy it. So, if you believe that you need the Saviour, and that Jesus Christ is the Saviour, and you want to be saved, then *make the decision* and tell Him so! Write this date in the flyleaf in your Bible to remember each year as the most important day in your life.

Reader, when did you receive Christ? Do you know? Why not? Isn't it important to you? Or is it that you have never done so yet? Will you accept Him and His love right now? Then "the God of love and peace shall be with you. . . . The grace of the Lord Jesus Christ, and the love of God, and the communion of the Holy Ghost, [will] be with you" (II Cor. 13:11, 14).

III. What Are the Results of God's Love in Our Lives?

A. WE WILL LOVE OTHERS BECAUSE WE HAVE THE EXAMPLE OF GOD HIMSELF

I JOHN 4:11. "Beloved, if God so loved us, we ought also to love one another."

Our love is but an echo of God's great love for us. Genuine God-love is not natural to mankind, so it is only the love of God in us that begets God's kind of love for others.

"Beloved!" What a heart-warming word! God's unutterable love falls like a mantle upon those who love Him. "The love of God is shed abroad in our hearts by the Holy Ghost which is given us" (Rom. 5:5). With the grace and love of God poured out upon us, we cannot help but show love and graciousness to others, and to show love in desiring the salvation of others.

I JOHN 4:7. "Beloved, let us love one another: for love is of God; and every one that loveth is born of God, and knoweth God."

Here is the dividing line between truth and error: That

Our Valentine to God

I LOVE YOU

LOVE BEGETS LOVE !

teaching is erroneous which says that man must make himself eligible for the love of God by being moral and religious. But God's Word says, God saved us "not by works of righteousness which we have done, but according to his mercy" (Titus 2:5). We read in Ephesians 2:4-5 that "God, who is rich in mercy, for his great love wherewith he loved us, even when we were dead in sins, hath quickened us [made spiritually dead men alive]." God can make man righteous without man's help.

"That ye, being rooted and grounded in love, may be able to comprehend with all saints what is the breadth, and length, and depth, and height; and to know the love of Christ, which passeth knowledge, that ye might be filled with all the fulness of God" (Eph. 3:17-19).

This is four-dimensional love!

The breadth includes all people of all ages and all races. The length covers all time—past, present, and future. The depth reached down to the lowest criminal guilty of the vilest crime, and to you and me! The height raises us up all the way to the very presence of our holy God! Glory, hallelujah!

The Arrow pierces both hearts — ties them together!

I JOHN 3:16. "Because he laid down his life for us: . . . we ought to lay down our lives for the brethren."

As He so loved and gave, so we are to love and give. He gave His life on the cross, but we are to give our lives that others might know Him. To "lay down our lives" has the meaning of giving up our own selfish preferences and desires for the well-being of others. The natural, unsaved man lives only for himself—his own comforts and ambitions, his possessions, and his success. But if we love others, we will be willing to forsake our self-centered way of living in order that others may learn how to be saved. It is perhaps easier to give up one's life in one grand gesture in a martyr's death than to live a whole lifetime of self-abasement and patience among people whose dispositions and ungodliness seem unbearable; but this is the practical meaning of OTHERS FIRST. Love is life-giving: giving our life.

Perhaps someone is asking now, "How can I love someone who has hurt me and slandered me?" Much rather you ought to ask how God could love you and me with all our rebellion and shame! By ourselves, it is true, we have no

power to be victorious over our likes and dislikes; but the
power of God is available, and He will give us the love-
power to forgive and forget. After all, do we love ourselves so much that we can only be gracious and loving to
those that are attractive to us? Are we so self-centered that
we would rather hold a grudge than win others to Christ?
Sensitivity is a product of self-love. May God heal us!

B. WE WILL LOVE OTHERS BECAUSE WE ARE COMMANDED TO DO SO

I JOHN 4:21. "And this commandment have we from him,
    That he who loveth God love his brother also."

When we say we love God, we should also love those who
belong to Him. This is one of the outward proofs that we
are saved. Always remember that love of God and love of
man go together! No father is glad when his children do
not love one another, and the heavenly Father is no exception. He too, desires that His children walk in love, and
He has gone so far as to command it. Christians, are we

disobedient to this command? The love of God for us is to go through us to others.

Genuine love is not a whipped-up feeling of comraderie but rather a sincere desire for the well-being of our enemies as well as our friends, even as Christ prayed, "Father, forgive them; for they know not what they do" (Luke 23:34).

I John 5:1. "Every one that loveth him that begat loveth him also that is begotten of him."

Christ is called the only begotten Son, but this verse "him also that is begotten" refers rather to born-again ones. What a tremendous work God could do in the world if He could only trust the saved ones to love each other as they should!

It seems strange how some Christians would rather make friends and join up in religious union with those who are not true to the Word of God than cast their vote with the truth. Such are popularity-seekers, much like the Pharisees in Jesus' day, who "loved the praise of men more than the praise of God" (John 12:43). It is not love to fraternize with error and false doctrine, and it is not love to condone worldliness and sin. Unless our love makes us faithful in rebuking and warning, it is sheer sentimental emotionalism.

I John 3:11. "For this is the message that ye heard from the beginning, that ye should love one another."

This love is Christ's nature reproduced in us by the Holy Spirit, and it is sufficient for our home as well as for the church and those outside. Strange how we so often show our best side to outsiders, but make little effort to be courteous and considerate in the home. Those we should love the most, we often neglect or we tread over them roughshod. A wife says she loves her husband, but sometimes she may act as if she doesn't even like him. And the same can be said of husbands.

Oh, we would not think of killing someone; but we hate people and hatred is the same in the sight of God as murder. Sin is measured by the desire and the motive, and not just by the act. Those who do not love cannot be the children of God.

"Not as Cain, who was of that wicked one, and slew his brother. And wherefore slew he him? Because his own works were evil, and his brother's righteous" (I John 3:12). The sin of jealousy cannot remain with love; selfishness cannot abide with love; and hate cannot keep company with love. These were the sins of Cain. His was no spontaneous crime; it started with disobedience to God (when he offered the wrong kind of sacrifice), went on to jealousy, resentment, and then murder. He was religious; he had come to offer a sacrifice!

Unsaved people perform some kind and moral deeds, but they are still guilty of rejecting the Son of God. For instance, gangsters might be generous to their children; murderers might do nice things for the boys' club; thieves might give generously to benevolences.

In Jesus day, the scribes and Pharisees were religious zealots, with their fastings and prayers, but they shouted, "Crucify him! Crucify him!" when Pilate offered to release Him.

Judas was religious. He followed Jesus, and even preached and did miracles; but he was not a saved man. Although he returned the blood money, he never repented before God.

But we who are God's children are to love God and love others.

I JOHN 3:17. "But whoso hath this world's good and seeth his brother have need, and shutteth up his bowels of compassion from him, how dwelleth the love of God in him?"

What is this world's good? The things needful for spiritual and physical well-being.

If we have a knowledge of the Word of God, we are to give it out. If we have experienced the strength God gives against temptation, we are to encourage others by telling them how we have been helped. If we have plenty of material resources, and others are in dire straits, we are to share our abundance with them. When we have home and friends, and others are alone, we could include them in some of our family gatherings or invite them to luncheon or dinner. It is all just as practical as that! But how few Christians really practice love! How selfish we are!

I JOHN 3:18. "Let us not love in word, neither in tongue; but in deed and in truth."

It is easy to talk about love, and not put it into action.

Christians and church groups make so many plans to show love and win souls, and they are forever studying about how to do personal work and visit, but they seldom get around to doing anything about it. It's time to stop talking and get busy!

The primary work of the church is to snatch souls from the danger of eternal punishment, to save them from the power of sin in this life, rather than to work for world peace, or demonstrate for integration, or civic reform. Only spiritual revival can bring about any permanent reform.

In some churches you see Christians who cultivate personal friends and form cliques. They are indifferent to other Christians who may be lonely or in need of help. When the Scripture says, "Use hospitality one to another without grudging," and urges that one be "a lover of hospitality," it does not mean selfish entertainment only of personal friends and family! In Bible days, when there were no suitable hotels for travelers, the believers were expected to lodge Christian wayfarers without grudging, even though they were strangers.

The church is not a social club; it is the body of Christ! And the duties and privileges of a Christian life are to be practiced here and now, and not kept for another world! We are saints now, so we ought to be saintly!

Our love is to branch out into a five-branched tree:

1) Love to God.

2) Love to our family. A sentimental valentine cannot take the place of lack of courtesy and affection all the year around. Bickering and unloving parents make juvenile delinquents!

3) Love to other Christians, no matter what their social standing or attractiveness.

4) Love for our community. Its welfare should be our personal responsibility and not a project of the church.

5) Love for lost souls, that they might be brought to Christ. It is time to begin loving in truth.

I JOHN 4:20. "If a man say, I love God, and hateth his brother, he is a liar: for he that loveth not his brother whom he hath seen, how can he love God whom he hath not seen?"

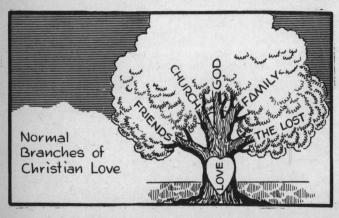

Normal Branches of Christian Love

A bitter and caustic woman who claims to be a Christian, told me she would not attend any church because there were so many hypocrites and enemies in them all. She just could not bring herself to sit in church and see them all so smug and religious and know that they did not live their religion at home.

"But why go to church to look at them?" I asked. "Surely there is something in the messages or in the reading or singing and praying that could feed your soul. Why look at and think about people? Why not think about the Lord? Surely you don't have anything against the Lord!"

You will never find a perfect group of people. But you can find churches where you will hear good messages from good pastors. And no matter how imperfect Christians are, they worship a perfect Lord. After all, if any congregation were perfect, there would be no need for preaching; and if it were perfect then the moment you or I joined it, it would be imperfect!

We must exercise and cultivate love. In fact, when the "I" in the word "live" is bent over in humility, then it becomes an "O" (zero, nothing!), and then we have the word

Let the "I" become "ZERO"

"love." Real love is when I am zero! And this is real living, too!

C. WE WILL LOVE OTHERS BECAUSE REAL LOVE SHOWS ITSELF

I JOHN 4:12. "No man hath seen God at any time. If we
love one another, God dwelleth in us, and his love is
perfected in us."

"God is a Spirit; and they that worship him must worship
him in spirit and in truth" (John 4:24). A spirit is not
material being, so it cannot be seen or comprehended by
physical means. Until we get to heaven, we must see God
through the love and character of Jesus Christ and through
the Word, and through the lives of those who belong to
Him. "No man hath seen God at any time; the only begotten Son, . . . he hath declared him" (John 1:18). Now
that Christ has returned to glory, we are the only Bible the
careless world will read; we are the sinner's Scriptures; we
are the scoffer's creed; To us Christ said, "Love one another; as I have loved you that ye also love one another.
By this shall all men know that ye are my disciples, if ye
have love one to another" (John 13:34-35).

It pays to advertise, and it is expensive too. God knows
this.

He has blazed across the centuries the most lavish and expensive advertising of all time. The background of this ad-
vertisement is a darkened sky and a fearful earthquake. In
the foreground is a shouting rabble of people, priests, and
soldiers. In the very center of the picture is a green hill
where a cross stands silhouetted between earth and heaven,
and on that cross is the Son of God. Himself! His love is
written in letters of His own blood. This is advertising
which surpasses all other advertising. "But God commend-

eth [advertises] his love toward us, in that, while we were yet sinners, Christ died for us" (Rom. 5:8).

God's love needs no perfecting, but when we love Him and love others, then our love is the final satisfaction and fulfillment of His love for us.

D. WE WILL LOVE OTHERS BECAUSE WE ARE "AS HE IS"

I JOHN 4:17. "Herein is our love made perfect, . . . because as he is, so are we in this world."

God has accepted us because we are *in Christ.* He sees us as belonging to the family, and one with Christ, and therefore we are to love as He loved. As Christ took rejection for us, we must be willing to suffer for Him. As He set aside His own will, so we should be willing to set aside our self-will. He came to seek and to save that which was lost; so we should be in this world as He is. He so loved that He gave; and we should so love that we give!

I JOHN 4:16. "And we have known and believed the love that God hath to us. God is love; and he that dwelleth in love dwelleth in God, and God in him."

The believer is in God, and God is in him. How a full realization of this should change our homes and habits! How can a Christian presume to continue in careless living and unkind behavior when he realizes he is the temple of God?

I knew a lady whose whole life was a poem of love and kindness, and her heart was as big as the great outdoors, even for her vicious and ungodly husband. God answered her prayers for his salvation after many years of violence and drunkenness, and they had a few years of joy in the Lord before they were both taken in sudden death.

But that funeral service was a triumph of praise, for all remembered her love and praise for the Lord even through all her years of misery. How her life had radiated Christ! Truly He indwelt her in all His fullness.

For faithful Christians, death is but "graduation day" on earth and "commencement day" in heaven! To be with Christ is far better, and the departed one has but one desire for those left behind—that they should glorify the Lord and rejoice in Him!

Graduation from earth —
Commencement in Glory !

I JOHN 4:18. "There is no fear in love; but perfect love
casteth out fear: because fear hath torment. He that
feareth is not made perfect in love."

Guilt and fear go together. When we know that we are
in Christ, and when we realize that "as he is, so are we,"
then we have no reason to fear. "The fear of the Lord,"
spoken of so often in the Bible, means respect, reverence
and awe, and not frightened terror. Believers do not fear
any future judgment, for "there is . . . no condemnation to
them which are in Christ Jesus" (Rom. 8:1).

God's Word tells us that in the last days men's hearts
shall fail them because of fear and for looking for the evil
things that shall come upon the earth. On every side we
meet people who are tormented by fears—fear of the unknown, of illness, of penury, of failure, of persecution, and
so on. The trouble, when we fear, is that our hearts are
not right with God. Fear is a way of saying we do not
trust God.

How can we fear when He has inspired such words as
these: "Hast thou not known? hast thou not heard, that the
everlasting God, the LORD, the Creator of the ends of the
earth, fainteth not, neither is weary? there is no searching
of his understanding. He giveth power to the faint; and to
them that have no might he increaseth strength. . . . But
they that wait upon the Lord shall renew their strength;
. . . He shall feed his flock like a shepherd: he shall gather
the lambs with his arm, and carry them in his bosom"
(Isa. 40:28-31, 11).

Shall He not care for us for whom Christ died?

"And we know that all things work together for good to
them that love God [or, God is working all things together
for good], to them who are the called according to his purpose [the purpose of salvation and holiness]. For whom he

THE ALMIGHTY CREATOR – –OUR SHEPHERD!

Isaiah 40:11-30

did foreknow [He knew before we were ever born], he also did predestinate [He planned our future even before the world was created]. . . . whom he justified, them he also glorified. . . . If God be for us, who can be against us? He that spared not his own Son, but delivered him up for us all, how shall he not with him also freely give us all things [safety, certainty, and enjoyment]? Who shall lay anything to the charge of God's elect? It is God that justifieth [shall God that justifieth?]. Who is he that condemneth? It is Christ that died [shall Christ Jesus who died?], yea rather, that is risen again, who is even at the right hand of God, who also maketh intercession for us" (Rom. 8:28-34).

Worried Christian, do you hear those words? Christ, who rose from the dead, is now interceding for us! How can you fear?

Remember, everything that comes to us as Christians comes from the hand of our loving Lord and, whether we like it or not, it is all for good.

When we were children, we might not have appreciated that bitter medicine that our mother made us take, but it came from her loving hand for our good! So in life's circumstances, let us keep our eyes off the big medicine spoon and on the blessed hand that is giving it to us for good!

We can have confidence instead of worry, joy instead of torment, peace instead of fear—and all because we know the love of Christ "which passeth all understanding."

There are several reason for God's "big medicine spoon" in life:

1. To bring the unsaved to God. Acts 9:1-16.
2. To keep the Christian close to Him. We are so independent of God when things go too well! Psalm 119:71, 75; 86:7.
3. To refine our character. We need more patience and trust and love. James 1:2-4; Job 23:10.
4. To give as a testimony that we would not have otherwise. I Peter 2:20; 4:12-19.
5. To glorify God, that others might see our life and want Him too. John 11:4; Colossians 1:24.
6. To receive comfort from God, so we might comfort others. II Corinthians 1:3-5.
7. To wean us from the things of the earth.

8. To chastise for sin. Hebrews 12:5-7; Job 5:17-18.
9. To receive when we get to glory, a special reward for enduring trials. James 1:12; I Peter 1:6-7.

IV. What We Are Not to Love

I JOHN 2:15-16. "Love not the world, neither the things that are in the world. If any man love the world, the love of the Father is not in him."

Here is the one "love not"! We are not to set our heart on the things of Satan's world system, and give such things the place that God should have in our lives. The world is anything that cools our affection for Christ—yes, even harmless things! Love misplaced robs God of His place. We do not have to give up wrong things, we simply give up ourselves! Then we may do what we like, because we like what He likes!

I JOHN 5:21. "Little children, keep yourselves from idols."

Set not your heart on anything but the Lord.

Do you really love Him? Here is an acid test, Christian, to find out just how much you do love God:

1. Do you think about God constantly? Is Christ in the center of your plans?
2. Do you delight in obedience to God; and is worship and prayer service your joy?
3. Is the Bible your sincere interest and do you read and study it daily?
4. Do you love other Christians? Or do you prefer unsaved friends?
5. Are you miserable when you sin, and do you confess and forsake it speedily?
6. Do you prefer to remain here on earth, or do you desire to be with the Lord?

7. Have you lost your first love for the Lord? Do you feel barren and cold?

The way back to God is by way of confession and contrition, and to say, as Peter said, "Lord, thou knowest all things; thou knowest that I love thee."

O the bitter pain and sorrow,
That a time could ever be
When I proudly said to Jesus,
"All of self and none of Thee!"

Yet He found me, I beheld Him,
Bleeding on th' accursed tree,
And my wistful heart said faintly,
"Some of self and some of Thee!"

Day by day His tender mercies,
Healing, helping, full, and free,
Brought me lower, while I whispered,
"Less of self, and more of Thee!"

Higher than the highest heavens,
Deeper than the deepest sea,

"Lord, Thy love at last hath conquered,
None of self and ALL OF THEE!"

QUESTIONS

1. What are the two sides of God's character? Romans 11:22.
2. To whom does God show mercy? Psalm 86:5.
3. Whom will God pardon? Isaiah 55:7.
4. Does God want men to perish? II Peter 3:9.
5. How does God love the believer? Ephesians 2:4; Psalm 86:15; John 17:23.
6. Why does God love the believer? John 16:27.
7. How do we know God remembers us? Isaiah 49:15-16.
8. Does God sympathize with our troubles? Isaiah 63:9.
9. How long does God's love last? Jeremiah 31:3.
10. How are husbands and wives to love each other? Ephesians 5:21-33.

5

GOD'S TRUTH ABOUT OBEDIENCE

ALL THE COMMANDS in the New Testament for lost sinners can be summarized in only one: "Ye must be born again!" However, this is something that self-sufficient sinners cannot accept. Their pride refuses to let them believe that God requires them to be born again, and they concoct a philosophy of self-effort which runs them into a blind alley of confusion. "There is a generation that are pure in their own eyes, and yet is not washed from their filthiness" (Prov. 30:12).

I. God's Command for the Unsaved

I JOHN 3:23. "And this is his commandment, That we should believe on the name of his Son Jesus Christ, and love one another, as he gave us commandment."

Any efforts at being good or doing religious deeds before coming to Christ for salvation are actually repulsive to God. "But we are all as an unclean thing, and all our righteousnesses are as filthy rags" (Isa. 64:6). Even our so-called good is rotten, filthy, and rejected! Today, even as in Jesus' time, people ask, "What shall we do, that we might work the works of God?" Jesus replied, "This is the work of God, that ye believe on him whom he hath sent" (John 6:28-29).

Suppose someone came to your house and beat and killed your son and then later rang your doorbell and in sugary tones asked to help you with your work. What would you

say? Yet that is what guilty sinners do when they offer their good works to God. God says to them, "You have rejected My Son, and I reject your work!"

It is only when we weigh the effect of sin that we can appreciate its poisonous character. Fond parents excuse their wayward children by saying, "My son is really good at heart!" It is pathetic to see their blinded love. But God's love isn't blind. He says all of the human race is very bad at heart. "The heart is deceitful above all things, and desperately wicked" (Jer. 17:9).

So then, the first and only command for lost sinners is to accept Christ as their personal Saviour. There must be spiritual life before there can be any acceptable deeds. You wouldn't think of placing a radio in a cemetery and tuning in on a program of setting-up exercises, would you? Everyone there is dead! No one can get "up and down" at all!

Sin is not misfortune; it is self-will, direct disobedience against God.

Strange as it may seem, men have even twisted the words "faith" and "trust" to mean something that they might do by their own efforts. They say, "Just believe hard enough, and all will be well! Have enough faith and things will work out!" Thus they have taken the matter of salvation back into their own hands. They think of their own efforts as "having faith." But saving faith is not just "willing it so," and neither is it thinking positive thoughts. Saving faith accepts the Saviour.

II. God's Command for the Believer

I JOHN 2:3. "And hereby do we know that we know him, if we keep his commandments."

God has not left us dangling; He does not leave us to guess just what His standard of Christian living is. We are saved by grace through faith, but we are to show our faith by obedience. We are justified before God by trusting Him, but we are justified before men by how we live. "Faith without works is dead."

Now, just what are the commands for the believer under this dispensation of grace?

God has given various sets of laws in the Bible. There is the perpetual obligation of moral law (of right and wrong), which even the heathen know instinctively although they have never had the Bible. Their conscience knows it is bad to kill and steal. "For when the Gentiles [heathen], which have not the law [the law of Moses], do by nature the things contained in the law, these, having not the law, are a law unto themselves; which shew the work of the law written in their hearts, their conscience also bearing witness, and their thoughts the mean while accusing or else excusing one another" (Rom. 2:14-15).

Adam and Eve had law. God said to them, "Thou shalt not . . . " So the laws of reason were engraved on man's heart long before the law of Moses was given.

There are laws of nature which, if broken, will bring

trouble. Put your hand in the fire, and you'll get burned; breathe under water, and you'll drown. All these laws continue from beginning of time to the end of time. Another timeless law is the law of sin and death: the "wages of sin is death." Break God's law, and you reap the death penalty. Through Adam, all mankind has practiced *evil works*.

Then, there is the law given to Israel through Moses, which includes civic, ceremonial, and moral laws (including the ten commandments), and which produced *law works*. When Jesus Christ died on Calvary, He completed and fulfilled all the requirements and penalties of the law of Moses, and when He cried out, "It is finished!" the old covenant (the old arrangement, the Old Testament) was completed and done away. The Mosaic laws are not for Christians. Oh, yes, some of the principles and commands are carried over in the New Testament for us today, but we do not obey any commands in the Old Testament unless they are repeated in the New Testament after the death of Christ. We might add here that the Bible speaks of *dead works*. These are deeds done by the unsaved in the hope of making themselves acceptable to God; and God hates such works.

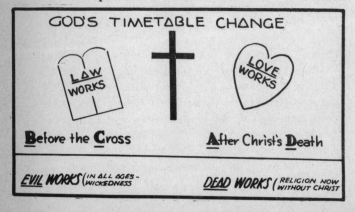

For the Christian, God's will is given in almost every chapter of the New Testament from the Gospel of John on to the end of the Bible. Obedience to these commands produces *love works, gracious works,* and *obedient works.*

The kind of works acceptable to God are those which are produced in the life of a Christian by the Holy Spirit. We read in Ephesians 2:10 that "we are his workmanship, created in Christ Jesus unto good works, which God hath before ordained that we should walk in them." These good works will be seen in the life of a Christian who obeys the will of God as he comes to know it through reading God's Word and listening to the voice of the Holy Spirit speaking to him through God's Word.

To disobey God's known will is sin. And one of John's purposes in writing this epistle is to let his readers know that, even though no Christian can claim he is sinless, God's purpose for the child of God is this: "that ye sin not."

I JOHN 2:1. "My little children, these things write I unto you, that ye sin not."

Christ is the Saviour not only from the penalty of sin but also from the domination of sin. The child of God has been born anew, so sin is a horror to him. He never boasts of his sin as he did before he was saved, for he no longer considers it clever or amusing; and he does not deliberately plan to sin, for he finds no joy in it.

In John 8 we read that Jesus turned to the woman taken in adultery, and said, "Go, and sin no more!" He says the same thing to us who have come to Him for salvation: "Sin not!" The heart gives homage to the Lord, and a complete transformation of life takes place, so that the converted person's bent of mind is toward holiness. God's righteousness in us should be a reality and not just a theological term. Holiness is to be through and through and not

just a shiny veneer. A real crisis must lead into a regular process, or it is mere empty emotion. You see, the preventive against sin is God Himself who indwells us. He "is able to keep you from falling" (Jude 24).

When an unsaved person sins, that is bad enough. But when a Christian sins, it is heartbreaking, for he is a traitor to God. If you say you are saved, then begin acting like it! God counts you righteous, so begin practicing righteousness! It is time to put salvation into practical operation!

Holiness includes the *motive* for obedience, and not just the actual deeds. Sometimes people are kept from doing wrong just because they are afraid of censure, or because they seek the praise of men, or because they are afraid of God's discipline. But we are dealing with the One who sees the innermost recesses of our hearts.

Going to church because it is our duty, singing in the choir because we want to show off our voice, teaching Bible classes to gain acclaim, or giving money to the church to avoid paying a higher income tax are certainly not holiness!

To be holy is to be what God wants you to be, to want

only what He wants, to do only what He would do. In other words, holiness is entire surrender of the self to Him! This is not a life-long, drab existence of subjugation to a despot but rather a joyful resurrection. Let go and let God! The act of sin is still possible to a believer, for he still has his old nature. But the habit of sin (when he runs freely and willingly to sin) is not possible to one who has been given a new nature (Eph. 4:22-24).

The abiding presence of the Holy Spirit is forever. "And I will pray the Father, and he shall give you another Comforter that he may abide with you for ever; even the Spirit of truth" (John 14:16-17). When we obey God, the things of the flesh that appealed to the old self shrivel up and lose their attractiveness, and spiritual things become supreme. Then we taste something of the peace and joy that God has promised.

Justifying faith also sanctifies. Spurious faith is mere words. ".What doth it profit, my brethren, though a man *say* he have faith, and have not works? can faith save him?" (James 2:14). The Greek meaning is, "Can *that* kind of faith save him?"

Too many so-called converts have never been converted in heart. To believe in the head only is dead orthodoxy. It is when we believe the truth with our whole heart that we experience salvation and begin to love God, and this will blossom out in love for others and a desire to walk with God. A true heart conversion prompts us to give our hands to serve Him, our mouth to speak for Him, and even causes us to reach down into our pocketbooks to give to Him! Something has really happened! Faith may be thought of as intangible, but it expresses itself in tangible ways.

Those who have faith will want to be faithful.

When molten lava from Mt. Vesuvius buried the city of Pompeii, a soldier was standing at his post in a niche next to the great gate. The excavations of that city reveal that this guard had not left his post even in the face of death. His remains still stand right there. Oh, that we might be as faithful to our King even in face of disaster! But instead we too often turn tail and run!

Let us consider now how obedience can be shown or demonstrated in the lives of Christians.

A. OBEDIENCE SHOWS ITSELF IN BIBLE STUDY

The gospel does not work by magic. We benefit from God's Word only when we know it and think upon it, and love and obey it. "Casting down imaginations, and every high thing that exalteth itself against the knowledge of God, and bringing into captivity every thought to the obedience of Christ" (II Cor. 10:5). Obedience is almost impossible to attain unless the mind is saturated with God's Word. In God's Word we learn what God wants us to do, and God's Word quickens and motivates us to do His will.

I JOHN 2:4. "He that saith, I know him, and keepeth not his commandments, is a liar, and the truth is not in him."

How important it is that we let the truth of God govern our lives! The "say-so" religion can often be a lie. Just to "say" we have faith does not prove our salvation. The Greek word translated "keepeth" in this verse can be translated "makes a practice of keeping" His commandments. So the teaching of this verse is that the person who makes a practice of *not* keeping God's commandments is a liar when he says he is a child of God. The truth is not in him.

The saved person may not always be faithful and obedient, but he *wants* to be! Thank God, even when we fail, we still belong to Him and He knows us! "The Lord knoweth them that are his. . . . Let every one that nameth the name of Christ depart from iniquity" (II Tim. 2:19).

A new bride might not be the best cook in the world, and may offer many a burnt offering to her patient husband (burnt on one side, and raw on the other!), but she is certainly trying! She is not perfect, but she is willing!

The one who claims to have been saved as a child, or some time ago, or even last week, but has no desire to obey God, is either a sad backslider or was never saved at all. He is a liar.

"Brethren, give diligence to make your calling and election sure: for if ye do these things, ye shall never fail: for so an entrance shall be ministered unto you abundantly into the everlasting kingdom of our Lord and Saviour Jesus Christ" (II Peter 1:10-11). What a warning this verse is! Are you sure you are really saved? God does the saving and does the calling and electing, it is true. But are you sure that you have responded? If you have, then you will want to obey Him, and obedience will keep you from falling into disrepute as a Christian; and you will have an abundant reward when you come into the presence of the Lord. You will hear Him say, "Well done, good and faithful servant!"

Are you sure you have been born again? Or are you just playing at Christianity?

I JOHN 2:5. "But whoso keepeth his word, in him verily is the love of God perfected: hereby know we that we are in him."

The words "the love of God" refer to our love of God. God's love needs no perfecting! Jesus said, "Ye are my friends, if ye do whatsoever I command you" (John 15:14).

In this verse the words "keepeth his word" have a deeper and richer meaning than just doing what we are actually commanded. Here the thought is to go beyond His stated commands, and seek to do His unexpressed will.

Suppose you left the house to do the shopping, and you told your son to cut the grass while you were gone. On your return, how pleased you would be to find he had mowed the lawn *and* trimmed the hedge! He knew it needed doing, and that you would like it done, although you had not said so. He had obeyed your command, and he had done your will. (However, most youngsters do as little as they can get away with! And so do Christians!)

One new Christian said to me, "Now I've read the Bible through, so what more is there to Christianity?"

Taking the Bible, we sat down together and read Ephesians 3, and I explained the verses as we read. After more than an hour of such reading and explanation, she looked up and said, "I still haven't scratched the surface of God's Word, have I?"

"No," I agreed, "we are all just like babies dabbling our toes in the froth of the wave that has just broken on the shore, and crying out, 'Look Mommy, I'm in the whole ocean!'"

"Study to shew thyself approved unto God, a workman that needeth not to be ashamed, rightly dividing the word of truth" (II Tim. 2:15). To *study* to be approved means to make it our *life occupation* to be approved unto God, an unembarrassed workman who knows how to interpret the Bible as well as how to obey it.

To keep God's Word, then, means to go the second mile with God. But most Christians fail miserably in showing their love for God, in letting their love of God be perfected in them in everyday living.

B. OBEDIENCE SHOWS ITSELF IN WORSHIP

Genuine worship consists of affection, appreciation, prayer, and response in obedience—all of which issue from knowing and understanding God. Worship is no mere form or ritual, but involves being occupied with God. In order to offer "worth-ship" to God we must ourselves be in "worthy shape," and disobedience immediately disqualifies us for fellowship with Him. "And let us consider one another to provoke unto love and good works: not forsaking the assembling of ourselves together, as the manner of some is; but exhorting one another: and so much the more, as ye see the day approaching" (Heb. 10:24-25). The "day" refers to Christ's return.

We are now so much closer to the coming of the Lord than when the Bible was written, so how much more important it is for us to gather together for worship and preaching and teaching than nineteen hundred years ago. But do we? Even fifty years ago Christians went to services twice or more on Sunday, and also to a midweek prayer meeting. But nowadays many Christians act as if they were doing God a favor to go to church once a week. Instead, they "gather together" around the family reunion dinner table and the television!

True worship stimulates our desire to stir ourselves up as well as others.

Sometimes a lazy Christian asks, "Can't I be a Christian and not go to church?"

"Yes, you can be a Christian and not go to church, but

you'll be a poor one! It's also possible to be a member of a family and never go home!"

Those who fight attending services are either lazy or backslidden; and they are disobeying God, and that is sin.

Gathering together to worship helps to keep us warm for God, harnesses our efforts for God, and safeguards us against backsliding from God. Mountain-climbers tie themselves together on dangerous climbs so that if one slips the others will hold him up. They need each other.

We, too, need to be tied up to a group of fellow believers, among whom we can serve and be served, and in whose fellowship we can be stirred up to love and good works.

C. OBEDIENCE SHOWS ITSELF IN GIVING

There was a tight-fisted man who defended his not giving to the Lord by saying, "The dying thief didn't have to give, and he went straight to paradise!"

His little son looked at him curiously for a moment, and then asked, "Pa, are you a dying thief?"

In one of His parables Christ told of a nobleman going off on a journey and telling his servants, as he gave each

of them an equal amount of money, "Occupy till I come."
Applied to Christians, this means to do business for Him
in the salvation of souls instead of just sitting in our old
rocker and waiting for Him to return!

But to do business for Him takes money as well as brawn.
The local church assembly is the business office for soul-
winning, but this has to be supported by the gifts of the
believers. We are to give according to our means. This is
the same principle that Uncle Sam uses in taxation, but the
difference is that when we give to God, He in turn rewards
sacrificial giving with manifold blessings, both in this life
and in the life to come (Mark 10:29-30). "Give, and it
shall be given unto you; good measure, pressed down,
shaken together, and running over, shall men give into
your bosom. For with the same measure that ye mete
withal it shall be measured to you again" (Luke 6:38).

God has promised to supply all our need *when*—and this
is often overlooked—we give to the work of the ministry.
It was to Christians who had helped Paul in his need that
he wrote, "But my God shall supply all your need according
to his riches in glory by Christ Jesus" (Phil. 4:19).

"Every man according as he purposeth in his heart, so let him give; not grudgingly, or of necessity: for God loveth a cheerful [hilarious and generous] giver. And God is able to make all grace abound toward you; that ye, always having all sufficiency in all things, may abound to every good work" (II Cor. 9:7-8). Giving is a good work. Can it be that you are not abounding in every good work? Every promise of God has two parts: His and yours. Don't expect to see all-sufficiency in all things unless you are giving!

D. OBEDIENCE SHOWS ITSELF IN LOVE

I JOHN 2:7. "Brethren, I write no new commandment unto you, but an old commandment which ye had from the beginning. The old commandment is the word which ye have heard from the beginning."

As we look behind the curtain of time, we see written across the face of eternity the one word "love." Jesus summarized all the Old Testament commandments in this way: "Thou shalt love the Lord thy God with all thy heart, and with all thy soul, and with all thy mind. This is the

first and great commandment. And the second is like unto
it, Thou shalt love thy neighbor as thyself. On these two
commandments hang all the law and the prophets" (Matt.
22:37-39).

Love sums up the New Testament commands: "And this
is his commandment, That we should believe on the name
of his Son Jesus Christ, and love one another, as he gave us
commandment" (I John 3:23).

We find the same principle in both the old and the new
covenants: Love God and love others. We do not need
new truths, just new understanding of the old ones.

A young man who considered himself an expert on psy-
chology told me that he had had his life all neatly patterned
until he started coming to my classes. "Now I just don't
know where to fit Jesus Christ into the pattern!"

"Don't try to fit Him into your pattern," I told him.
"You let Him fit you into His!"

I JOHN 2:8. "Again, a new commandment I write unto you,
    which thing is true in him and in you, because the
    darkness is past, and the true light now shineth."

Love is the fulfillment of the law for both the old and
the new dispensations, but it comes to us who live in the
new dispensation with fresh meaning and a wider sense of
obligation. We are far more responsible to love than those
in Moses' times. We have a new example of love in the
Lord Jesus Christ, and we are indwelt by the Holy Spirit,
who is willing to produce Christ's love in us. The darkness of ignorance is past, and the guilt of our sin has been
removed. We can know more of Him and act more like
Him—all because He is in us.

We are to KNOW, GROW. GLOW, and GO for Christ!

TELL SOMEONE ELSE!

Just as luminous paint must be exposed to light if it is to glow in the dark, so the Christian must be exposed to the light of the love of Christ constantly if he is to glow in the darkness of sin and hate. God says, "Ye are all the children of light, and the children of the day: we are not of the night, nor of darkness. Therefore let us not sleep, as do others; but let us watch and be sober, . . . But let us who are of the day, be sober, putting on the breastplate of faith and love; and for an helmet, the hope of salvation. For God hath not appointed us to wrath, but to obtain salvation by our Lord Jesus Christ. Who died for us, that, whether we wake or sleep, we should live together with him" (I Thess. 5:5-10).

I JOHN 2:9. "He that saith he is in the light, and hateth his brother, is in darkness even until now."

John again uses the expression "he that saith." He is making it very evident that just because a person says he is in the light does not make it so. This is the condition of the unsaved person who is still in darkness but who thinks he is a Christian. Such a person is still in darkness and is in great danger. He does not see the precipice, the enemy lurking, and fearful horrors unknown. Light shows up all such dangers, but ungodly men love darkness rather than light, because their deeds are evil. "For every one that doeth evil hateth the light, neither cometh to the light, lest his deeds should be reproved" (John 3:20).

Years ago, the British crown sent messengers to the Bahamas to show goodwill and keep the favor of their colony. They offered to grant any request that the islands might desire. The answer was quick in forthcoming, "Tear down all the lighthouses!" Why? The main occupation of the Bahamas was salvaging. The lighthouses ruined their business because they prevented shipwrecks.

Jesus said, "I am the light of the world: he that followeth me shall not walk in darkness, but shall have the light of life" (John 8:12).

I JOHN 2:10. "He that loveth his brother abideth in the light, and there is none occasion of stumbling in him."

Anyone who loves God and loves others lives in the light;

LIGHT SHOWS UP
THE ROCKS

he does not stumble, neither does he cause others to stumble over him. It is the unloving and disobedient Christian that drives men away from seeking God. We like to blame the pastor or the officers of the church when no souls are being saved, but it is more likely our own unfaithfulness and lack of love that people see. And they don't like what they see!

I JOHN 4:21 "And this commandment have we from him, that he who loveth God love his brother also."

Love is to be practiced as well as professed. "That their hearts might be . . . knit together in love" (Col. 2:2). The hearts of believers are knit together in love as they fellowship together in the Lord and give comfort, cheer, and encouragement to each other. As love is the right climate for raising a happy Christian family, so love is also the hothouse for a happy church family in the Lord. A loving family will not want "roast preacher" for Sunday dinner! Some parents have complained that their children lost interest in church as they grew older. But could it be that their children got fed up with hearing church quarrels discussed in the home? "Little pitchers have big ears!"

Christian parents whose relationships indicate a lack of love toward one another will raise rebellious children. They will always remember how mother and dad spoke to each other, and they will remember the coolness between their parents, and looks like daggers. Even some Christian homes are raising monsters! And why? Because the parents are monsters too! Lack of love is an abnormal Christian trait, and to be abnormal is to be a freak and monster! How God must yearn over us that we might be normal and healthy!

E. OBEDIENCE SHOWS ITSELF IN POWER IN PRAYER

I JOHN 3:22. "And whatsoever we ask, we receive of him, because we keep his commandments, and do those things that are pleasing in his sight."

Our prayer power depends on our obedience to God. Real prayer is communion with God Himself, and all His blessings are but means to making us what He wants us to be. "The LORD is nigh unto all them that call upon him, to all that call upon him in truth. He will fulfil the desires of them that fear him: he also will hear their cry, and will save them" (Ps. 145:18-19).

In sad contrast, God does not promise to grant requests to those who have rejected Christ. The only prayer He will answer for them is their prayer for salvation. All other prayers of the unsaved are repulsive to Him. "The sacrifice of the wicked is an abomination to the LORD: but the prayer of the upright is his delight . . . The LORD is far from the wicked: but he heareth the prayer of the righteous" (Prov. 15:8, 29).

People seem to have the idea—an erroneous one—that God

will hear everybody's prayers, no matter how they have flaunted Him. But He says, "Because I have called, and ye refused; I have stretched out my hand, and no man regarded; but ye have set at nought all my counsel, and would none of my reproof: I also will laugh at your calamity; . . . Then shall they call upon me, but I will not answer; they shall seek me early, but they shall not find me" (Prov. 1:24-28).

Superstition looks on prayer as some sort of Aladdin's lamp that will bring whatever people want. And when they don't get their answer, such people fall apart emotionally and accuse God of failing them.

"Behold, the LORD'S hand is not shortened, that it cannot save; neither his ear heavy, that it cannot hear: but your iniquities have separated between you and your God, and your sins have hid his face from you, that he will not hear" (Isa. 59:1-2).

To receive answers to prayer, we must meet two conditions: first, we must belong to God by faith in Christ Jesus; and second, we must do that which is pleasing in His sight. "The eyes of the Lord are over the righteous, and his ears are open unto their prayers" (I Peter 3:12). Prayer not only changes things but people—and that means you and me! Prayer changes us by changing our attitudes so that we leave our burdens with God instead of dictating to Him how to solve them.

If you are in a small boat which is tied to a dock, and you pull on the rope, the dock does not come closer to you; you come closer to the dock! So, when we pull on the rope of prayer, it draws us closer to His will, and does not force Him to do our will. We Christians ought to feel ashamed that we neglect the privilege of prayer as we do.

"Praying *always* with *all* prayer and supplication in the Spirit, and watching thereunto with *all* perseverance and supplication for *all* saints" (Eph. 6:18). Notice that this prayer is *for* all saints, and not *to* all saints!

Power in prayer depends upon continuous obedience and fellowship. When prayer is not answered, it is not God's fault, but ours. "If I regard iniquity in my heart, the LORD will not hear me" (Ps. 66:18). All prayer that reaches God will be answered; either He will say "Yes" or "Not now" or "Something better." Just leave the answering to Him!

I JOHN 5:14. "And this is the confidence that we have in him, that, if we ask any thing according to his will, he heareth us."

Our confidence is "in Him," in the Almighty God, who is "able to do exceeding abundantly above all that we ask or think, according to the power that worketh in us" (Eph. 3:20). This is the all-powerful One whose hand is moved by the simple prayer of the humblest saint!

PRAYER MOVES THE HAND OF GOD

God is honored and glad when we have confidence in Him. Distrust dishonors Him. As sons of God, we have a direct line to the throne of glory, and yet how seldom we pick up the phone and call in! "Ye have not, because ye ask not."

However, it is well that we do not confuse faith in prayer with presumption and self-will. To ask "in faith believing" does not mean you try to dictate to God; neither does it mean you try to force the will of God, thinking that if you just ask hard enough you will get what you want. The person who prays in faith has implicit trust in God's love. wisdom, and power, and is willing for His will, even though it might mean denial of the petitions presented. His denials are for your good.

"Cast thy burden upon the LORD, and he shall sustain thee: he shall never suffer the righteous to be moved" (Ps. 55:22). This is our "cast and carry" promise! We cast, and He carries!

To say, "Thy will be done," does not mean as so many feel, "All hope is gone!" So often we use that petition as a sort of "last rites" after we have tried everything else.

A lady said, "The Bible says that God will give us the desires of our heart. So why don't I get what I want?" The Bible says, "Delight thyself also in the LORD; and he shall give thee the desires of thine heart" (Ps. 37:4-5). You see, that promise is conditional, as all the promises of God are. The condition for receiving the desires of our hearts is to delight ourselves in the Lord. When we delight ourselves in the Lord, then His will is our will, and we get what we want because we want what He wants! The "I" must be crucified. Only then can you and I say, "Not I, but Christ." Then my way becomes His way.

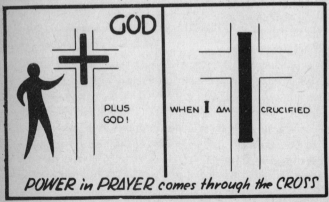

POWER in PRAYER comes through the CROSS

Imagine leaving a child in a doctor's office to play with the instruments and drugs! What a sad plight he would soon be in! And yet, we sometimes demand of God what we think *we* would like, and it might be just as harmful to us as those drugs to that child.

A certain father demanded that God heal his young son. He prayed for his healing with what he thought was the prayer of faith. There was no thought as to whether his petition might be God's will or not. The boy recovered, but years later died in the electric chair, blaspheming God. It would have been far better if he had gone to be with the Lord as a little child!

"And whatsoever ye shall ask in my name, that will I do, that the Father may be glorified in the Son. If ye shall ask any thing in my name, I will do it" (John 14:13-14). Christ's name is not to be used like some lucky charm; and neither do the words "We ask this in Jesus' name" make the petition according to His will. To ask in Christ's name implies complete surrender to the will of God, regardless of what it may mean. In order to pray like this, self-infatuation and lust and greed must be crucified with Christ. Then you will have real power in prayer! Feeble prayer is caused by a feeble life and feeble trust.

I JOHN 5:15. "And if we know that he hear us, whatsoever we ask, we know that we have the petitions that we desired of him."

Here is confidence in prayer! Here is rest from frustration! Now it is time to start praising! Faith produces praise, and praise brings answers: it is a glorious circle! Praiselessness is sin even as prayerlessness is sin. Thanks-giving and thanks-living preclude despondency; we will worship instead of worrying.

God says, "In nothing be anxious [don't worry about anything whatsoever], but in everything by prayer and supplication with *thanksgiving* let your requests be made known unto God" (Phil. 4:6, A.S.V.). God also says, "Call upon me in the day of trouble: I will deliver thee, and thou shalt glorify me. . . . Whoso offereth praise glorifieth me" (Ps. 50:15, 23). Praise is an offering, and praise born of trust can be offered even before the answer comes!

F. OBEDIENCE SHOWS ITSELF IN WALKING AS HE WALKED

I JOHN 2:6. "He that saith he abideth in him ought also to walk, even as he walked."

How did Jesus walk? He walked in the light. He walked in love. He went about doing good (Acts 10:38). He was in the place of worship on the day of rest. He knew the Word of God; He loved God; He loved souls; He prayed much, He was righteous. He gave Himself for others. This is how He walked.

It is easy to *talk* a Christian testimony, but there must be the *walk* to back up the talk. "Walk worthy of the Lord unto all pleasing [in all things pleasing to God], being fruitful in every good work, and increasing in the knowledge of God" (Col. 1:10). We are to please Him through and through. We should do away with all sham and hypocrisy!

"Can two walk together, except they be agreed" (Amos 3:3)? "As ye have therefore received Christ Jesus the Lord, so walk ye in him: rooted and built up in him and established in the faith" (Col. 2:6-7a).

We cannot walk as Christ walked unless we are seeing Him daily in the Word of God and meeting Him in prayer. Can you imagine my offering to paint your portrait if I had never seen you and had never seen your photograph? You would think I was crazy, and you'd be right! I'd have to see you often and spend time gazing at you in order to catch your likeness and put it on canvas.

The Christian experiences not only a change of family when he is converted but a change of living. If there is no change, perhaps there was no conversion. To "convert" is to change.

After the last world war, the United States army jeeps left behind in the Philippines were converted into public conveyances called jeepneys. As many as fifteen people with all their market produce could pile into one of these overworked "shuttle-bugs"! But the jeeps had to be converted before they could be used in this way. Conversion changed their appearance, their occupation, and their capacity!

Three things are involved in a successful Christian walk in obedience to God: sound doctrine (the head knowing the truth), receiving Christ (the heart knowing the Lord), walking as Christ walked (the practice knowing His fellowship). All three must stand together. This is no hop-skip-and-jump way of life; no pogo-stick progress of up and down and then lie down and take a vacation! This is step by step,

day by day, year by year, walking with Him and in Him and
for Him.

III. God's Commands Are Not Impossible

I JOHN 5:3. "This is the love of God, that we keep his commandments: and his commandments are not grievous."

To keep God's commandments is not impossible, nor is
it unreasonable. Christ told us, "My yoke is easy, and my
burden is light" (Matt. 11:30). He takes the heavy end,
and leaves the light to us. It is only when we are in step
with Him that we can carry the load of Christian responsibility. Harmony removes any irritation. When we feel the
commands of God are irksome, it shows we are out of step
with Him. The nurse does not resent abrupt orders from
the operating surgeon; she knows they are doing a work of
life and death together. How much more vital is our work
of life and death for lost souls!

I JOHN 5:21. "Little children, keep yourselves from idols."

Disobedience is a way of saying to God, "I care not what
You want or what You say; I want to go my own way!"
Such self-pleasing is sheer idolatry. We are just as sinful
and far more responsible than the heathen who make their
gods of wood and "cry unto the gods unto whom they offer
incense." Of those gods, the Lord said, "They shall not
save them at all in the time of their trouble." God told the
Prophet Jeremiah, "Therefore pray not thou for this people,
neither lift up a cry or prayer for them: for I will not hear
them in the time that they cry unto me for their trouble"
(Jer. 11:14).

It is surprising how even Christians neglect and disobey
God in utter disregard for His known will, and then when
they get into trouble, they come whimpering back to Him.

Thank His holy name, He is willing to take us back and forgive and cleanse us. But, oh, the wasted years and the hurt we have brought Him, and the discipline we have had to experience from His hand!

How much better to walk as He walked!

My new life I owe to Thee,
Jesus, Lamb of Calvary,
Sin was canceled on the tree,
Jesus, blessed Jesus!

Humbly at Thy cross I'd stay;
Jesus keep me there I pray;
Teach me more of Thee, each day,
Jesus, blessed Jesus!

Grant me wisdom, grace and pow'r,
Lord, I need Thee ev'ry hour;
Let my will be lost in Thine,
Jesus, blessed Jesus!

Saviour, Thou hast heard my plea,
Thou art near—so near to me;
Let me feel Thy strength'ning pow'r,
Jesus, blessed Jesus!

QUESTIONS

1. What is the source and result of saving faith? Ephesians 2:8-10.

2. Can those without saving faith please God? Hebrews 11:6.

3. Why study the Bible? John 5:39.

4. How often should we pray? Colossians 4:2.

5. Why should we be holy? I Corinthians 3:16-17; 6:11, 19-20.

6. How do we know Moses' laws are not for Christians? Galatians 3:19, 24-25.

7. What is the practical meaning of love? I Corinthians 13:1-8.

8. How can we love in deed and truth? Galatians 6:2.

9. How can we have peace in trial? Philippians 4:4-8.

10. What power do we have to obey God? Philippians 2:13.

6

GOD'S TRUTH ABOUT VICTORY

RATHER THAN SHUTTING the barn door after the horse has escaped, Christians should be on guard against the enemy of their souls before he hoodwinks them into believing the lies which he invents. Otherwise they will be as foolish as the person who leaves the barn door open and doesn't shut it until after the horse escapes.

I. Who Is the Enemy?

Originally, Satan was the most powerful of all God's created angels. He is a real being, and not just an evil force or influence. There can be no influence of good or evil without personality.

When Satan sinned by wanting to be God, he was cast down from the presence of God and became the archenemy of all good. He has been working overtime ever since to keep men from God and trip up Christians so that they become a poor testimony for the Lord. He is called the "accuser of the brethren," accusing them before God day and night (Rev. 12:9-10).

Can't you see his tactics? He tempts a Christian and trips him up, then turns and points his finger at them, shouting, "See! That's one of God's people! See what he did!"

How grateful we are that we believers have an Advocate with the Father, Jesus Christ the righteous! Also, He indwells us by His Spirit and "greater is he that is in you than he that is in the world" (I John 4:4). The devil is inferior to God, for he is only a created being and not the Creator. Satan is not all-powerful or all-knowing or everywhere at the same time. He is limited to the permissive will of God, and can only do what God permits.

Sometimes the question is asked, "Then why does God let the devil continue his wicked work?" We poor humans ask many questions, but God has not chosen to tell us the reasons for every thing He does or allows. "The secret things belong unto the LORD our God: but those things which are revealed belong unto us and to our children" (Deut. 29:29). However, we do know that in order for man to exert his will, he must make responsible choices. God desires us to love Him because we *want* to, and not because we are mere puppets that obey because we *have* to. So the devil's temptations serve as occasions when we choose either to obey God or disobey Him.

I JOHN 3:8. "The devil sinneth from the beginning."

Sin originated with Satan. He is the king of the wicked angels that fell with him, for Jesus said, "If Satan . . . be divided against himself, how shall his kingdom stand? because ye say that I cast out devils through Beelzebub" (Luke 11:18)   Several names are given to our archenemy: Lucifer, Beelzebub, Satan, the devil. "He was a murderer from the beginning, and abode not in the truth, because there is no truth in him. When he speaketh a lie, he speaketh of his own: for he is a liar, and the father of it" (John 8:44).

This is our enemy. Do not underestimate him! But don't overestimate him, either, for he is so very far inferior to Almighty God!

II. Who Are the Enemy's Helpers?

A. DEMONS

Because the devil is limited in power, he has to use helpers, called demons, to aid him in his dastardly work of keeping men from God. These wicked spirits are assigned

to know mankind, and to be familiar with the deeds and words and habits of those they tempt. The Bible calls them "familiar spirits" (Deut. 18:11). It is through these helpers that Satan rules, for there are legions of them and they seek to occupy and control the minds of the unsaved. "And when the unclean spirit is gone out of a man, he walketh through dry places, seeking rest, and findeth none. Then he saith, I will return to my house from whence I came out" (Matt. 12:43-45). Demons tempt Christians but cannot occupy them. Since the Holy Spirit indwells believers, they can never be demon-possessed.

B. THE ANTICHRIST

This is the wicked king that represents Satan during the Great Tribulation period that follows this Age of Grace. He will be a mock Christ (a counterfeit Christ), and will take over the whole earth by Satan's power after the saved ones have been caught away to be with Christ at the Rapture. He will not be revealed until the saints are gone (II Thess. 2:1-12). Daniel prophesies of this prince that shall come, and Paul calls him the "man of sin," but it is John that calls him the name of "the beast," and the "antichrist."

I JOHN 2:18. "Ye have heard that antichrist shall come."

This "beast" will be the adversary of Christ, the Messiah. He will tie up the whole world in a threefold dictatorship—political, economic, and religious. Politically, all nations will be under his one-world rule. Economically, all labor and business will be under his one-world control so that no man can buy or sell without his mark. Religiously, there will be a one-world church (not the Church of Jesus Christ, which has already gone to glory, but one combining all apostate religions) which will eventually be forced to wor-

ANTICHRIST

ECONOMICS | RELIGION | POLITICS

ONE WORLD

SATANIC LIES

PATCHING IT TOGETHER!

ship the Antichrist himself. The beast's name of antichrist indicates that he is against Christ. As a superman who is the embodiment of evil and lies, he will oppose Christ and offer himself instead of Christ. Thank God, the Christians will already have been raptured, and will not be on the earth when this antichrist appears!

The Antichrist will be cast into the lake of fire when Christ returns to the earth after the Great Tribulation to set up His kingdom in Jerusalem.

C. FALSE TEACHERS, OR MANY ANTICHRISTS

I JOHN 2:18. "Little children, it is the last time: and as ye have heard that antichrist shall come, even now are there many antichrists; whereby we know that it is the last time."

Even now in this age, Satan controls many men who deny Christ and aid him in keeping others from God. John had lived through a long period which began with the message of John the Baptist, and was now ending with God's last revelations through John himself. The world he had known was passing away; Jerusalem had fallen, the work of writing the New Testament was now being completed.

John had seen many who denied that Christ was really God and consequently had turned many away from the "faith once delivered to the saints."

Such antichrists have been in the world down through the ages since John. Antichrists are a present reality, but there will come in the future one person known as *the* Antichrist.

I JOHN 2:19. "They went out from us, but they were not of us."

The one test of truth and error is the Word of God. John's main message in all his writings is that Christ is truly God. Among those who left the assembly of the early Christians were those who denied that Christ was God. Peter prophesied that similar conditions would prevail in the last days of this Age as well as in the lifetime of the believers to whom he wrote: "But there were false phophets among the people, even as there shall be false prophets among you, who privily shall bring in damnable heresies, even denying the Lord that bought them and bring upon

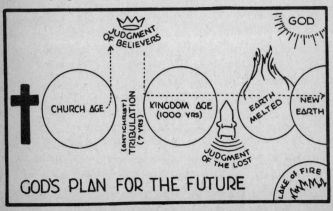

GOD'S PLAN FOR THE FUTURE

themselves swift destruction. And many shall follow their pernicious ways; by reason of whom the way of truth shall be evil spoken of" (II Peter 2:1-2). "Knowing this first, that there shall come in the last days scoffers, walking after their own lusts, and saying, Where is the promise of his coming?" (II Peter 3:3-4).

I JOHN 2:22. "Who is a liar but he that denieth that Jesus is the Christ? He is antichrist, that denieth the Father and the Son."

Jews and Gentiles alike understood the term "Jesus is the Christ" to mean that He was indeed "the Anointed One, the Holy One of Israel," and this was God. "For I am the LORD thy God, the Holy One of Israel, thy Saviour" (Isa. 43:3). It was Peter in the power of the Spirit who told the unbelieving Jews, "The God of Abraham, . . . hath glorified his Son Jesus; whom ye delivered up, and denied him in the presence of Pilate, . . . But ye denied the Holy One and the Just, and desired a murderer to be granted unto you" (Acts 3:13-14).

I JOHN 2:19. "If they had been of us, they would no doubt have continued with us: but they went out, that they might be made manifest that they were not all of us."

Here is the dividing of the wheat from the tares, the sifting of the chaff from the kernel. Those who belong to God may fall into sin, but they never deny that Christ is God. Those of whom the Apostle John wrote were showing that they had never belonged to God at all. This does not mean that a saved person can be lost. Those who belong to God are always in the family of God, and those who belong to His Church are *always* in His Church.

This seceding was a blessing in disguise, for it helped to purify the assembly of believers and to show the difference between the true and the false who had been concealed in the congregation. And perhaps no one realized what damage they had been doing.

How true this is even today! Jesus said, "Not every one that saith unto me, Lord, Lord, shall enter into the kingdom of heaven; but he that doeth the will of my Father which is in heaven. Many will say to me in that day, Lord, Lord, have we not prophesied in thy name? and in thy name cast out devils [demons]? and in thy name done many wonderful works? And then will I profess unto them, I never knew you: depart from me, ye that work iniquity" (Matt. 7:21-23).

There are those who insist that we should not separate from error and apostasy now but should rather work together with all religions until the time when Christ comes to judge. They use the parable of the wheat and tares as a basis for their reasoning (Matt. 13:24-30). But how wrong they are! Jesus was not advocating that the true believers and the false work together in spiritual union! He was simply bringing out the fact both would be in the world until God divided them for judgment. To be in the same world is quite different from working in the same spiritual harness!

Christ, John, Peter, Paul, and Jude all warn against allowing the leaven of error to remain in the gathering of cooperating believers. Today unsaved people should be urged to attend the meetings of the church to hear the Word of God, but not to work for God. The separation from liberal and wrong doctrine is not isolationism from seeking souls but is rather separation from cooperation with those who do not hold the "whole counsel of God." "Be ye not unequally yoked together with unbelievers: . . . Wherefore come out from among them, and be ye separate, saith the Lord" (II Cor. 6:14-17).

Those who are not true to God's Word are undercover agents for the devil. They camouflage their insidious heresies as they seek to turn others to their error. Often they use the local churches as bases of operation for their false preaching. "Neither give place to the devil" (Eph. 4:27). Don't give the enemy headquarters in Christ's camp!

God's order is not cooperation with unbelievers but separation. "If any man teach otherwise, and consent not to wholesome words, even the words of our Lord Jesus Christ, and to the doctrine which is according to godliness; . . . from such withdraw thyself" (I Tim. 6:3-5).

A young couple, newly converted, and suddenly involved in Christian leadership, was invited to attend our classes on the book of Revelation. They said, "No, we don't want to know anything about judgment or the wrath of God; we only want to know the message of the love of God!" It was a case of novices taking the lead in spiritual things before they knew the whole counsel of God. Truth is not part truth. We have no choice as to what we will accept or what we will reject. All of the Bible is the Word of God. When studying the Bible, we cannot do as we do with a pie—help ourselves to one piece, and leave the rest!

I JOHN 2:26. "These things have I written unto you concerning them that seduce you."

It is the work of Satan's helpers (demons and false teachers) to lure even the Christians into doubt and error, if possible. The devil is quite willing that men have religion, just as long as they do not accept the whole truth of the Bible. Part truth serves his purposes.

When a choice between truth and unity confronts us, we had better choose truth. "Buy the truth and sell it not." God warns against so-called preachers who have not been sent with His message. "I have not sent these prophets, yet they ran: I have not spoken to them, yet they prophesied. But if they had stood in my counsel, and had caused my people to hear my words, then they should have turned them from their evil way, and from the evil of their doings. . . . He that hath my word, let him speak my word faithfully" (Jer. 23:21-28).

The New Testament gives this exhortation: "Earnestly contend for the faith which was once delivered unto the saints. For there are certain men crept in unawares, . . . denying the only Lord God, and our Lord Jesus Christ" (Jude 3-4). Such men are like the man who embraces his friend while he is picking his pocket.

He greets his friend —
and picks his pocket!

I JOHN 4:1. "Beloved, believe not every spirit, but try the spirits whether they are of God: because many false prophets are gone out into the world."

It is neither love nor spirituality to ignore error. True love will try to enlighten and inform, and will not co-operate with evil. Spirituality is not stupidity! To discern is to use the sense God has given us to separate truth from error. "To the law and to the testimony: if they speak not according to this word, it is because there is no light in them" (Isa. 8:20).

God commands us to judge and discern. "For many deceivers are entered into the world, who confess not that Jesus Christ is come in the flesh. This is a deceiver and an antichrist . . . If there come any unto you, and bring not this doctrine, receive him not into your house, neither bid him God speed: for he that biddeth him God speed is partaker of his evil deeds" (II John 7, 10-11). How much more clearly does God have to speak?

I JOHN 4:2. "Hereby know ye the Spirit of God: Every spirit that confesseth that Jesus Christ is come in the flesh is of God."

"Spirits" refers to teachers: All people are spirits in human form.

I JOHN 4:3. "And every spirit that confesseth not that Jesus Christ is come in the flesh is not of God: and this is the spirit of antichrist, whereof ye have heard that it should come; and even now already is it in the world."

Error always rides on the back of truth; so there is no truth without counterfeit, and there is no error that does not have some truth. "Behold, the days come, saith the Lord GOD, that I will send a famine in the land, not a famine of bread, nor a thirst for water, but of hearing the words of the LORD. . . they shall run to and fro to seek the word of the LORD, and shall not find it" (Amos 8:11-12).

In Amos' day, God sent the famine of His Word, but today many nominal Christians are starving spiritually because they do not want true teaching. "The prophets prophesy falsely, . . . and my pople love to have it so" (Jer. 5:31). Such people are satisfied with the spiritual reducing diet of skim milk and hard tack, and wonder why they have no power in prayer, and so little knowledge of the Bible. They prefer the "church of their choice" instead of the "church of God's choice!"

"If any man speak, let him speak as the oracles of God [a divine revelation]; if any man minister, let him do it as of the ability which God giveth: that God in all things may be glorified through Jesus Christ, to whom be praise and dominion for ever and ever. Amen" (I Peter 4:11). The *message* is the truth; the *means* is the God-given ability; the *motive* is to glorify God!

III. The Enemy's Methods

A. DENYING SIN

I JOHN 1:8, 10. "If we say we have no sin, we deceive ourselves, and the truth is not in us. . . . If we say that we
have not sinned, we make him a liar, and his word is
not in us."

Here is the old adage, "Oh, you're not so bad! Everyone's
doing it! You're only human after all!" And the devil's
emissaries use the same argument, "There's good in everyone. . . . We all have a divine spark. . . . God will never
send anyone to hell. . . . Just do the best you can!"

The mind misled will take the affections and discernment
astray. How sinners eat up error! And how they avoid the
truth like the plague!

B. INDIFFERENCE

I JOHN 5:19b. "The whole world lieth in wickedness."

These words could be rendered: "The whole world is
rocked to sleep in the arms of the wicked one." Satan is

coddling the sinful human race and soothing their warped consciences, and lulling them to sleep in false security, when all the time he knows they will spend eternity with him in the lake of fire. Lost souls are presently in a stupor of indifference not realizing that if they continue in this state of indifference to Christ, eventually they will go to this place of eternal separation from God. Oh, that Christians might wake up this old world, before it is too late!

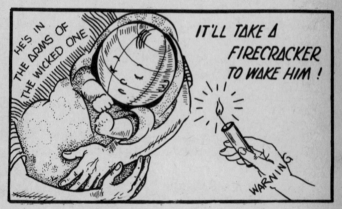

C. WORLDLINESS

I JOHN 2:16. "For all that is in the world, the lust of the flesh, and the lust of the eyes, and the pride of life, is not of the Father, but is of the world."

Until the unsaved are completely asleep in Satan's control, he dangles the baubles of the world before them (like bright toys before a baby), and they grasp for them instead of the things of God and eternity. Satan is a clever one, for he even uses this tactic upon the children of God! He knows who the carnal Christians are. He offers things that are passing away, things that cannot be taken away from this world—anything—in his efforts to keep men from seeking God.

Worldliness comes in three forms: attachment to outward things, attachment to transient things, and attachment to *any thing* ahead of God. To consider anything that hinders spiritual growth as absolutely necessary for our happiness, is to make that thing our god.

D. PERSECUTION

I JOHN 3:1. "The world knoweth us not, because it knew him not."

I JOHN 3:13. "Marvel not, my brethren, if the world hate you."

Now, if the Christian does not yield to the temptation of worldly attractions, Satan will apply persecution. Through troubles and persecutions he tempts Christians to become discouraged. Discouragement is one of his best tools. Satan and his helpers hate the child of God as much as they hate God, and down through the ages Christians have had to give their lives for testimony. But how far away such martyrdom is from the minor oppositions that send us running and yelping like a yellow cur! A smattering of criticism, or a smidgeon of ridicule, and we go into isolation, and are all ready to crown ourselves with a martyr's crown! How the devil's lip must curl in a sneer as he sees self-pity and cowardliness in Christians. "Ye have not yet resisted unto blood, striving against sin" (Heb. 12:4). And we talk about persecution!

John the Baptist was beheaded for his testimony. Tradition tells us Matthew was killed by the sword in Ethiopia; Mark was dragged through the streets until dead; Peter was crucified upside down; James was beheaded in Jeru-

salem; James the Less was thrown from the pinnacle of the temple, and then beaten to death; Philip was hanged; Bartholomew was flayed alive; Andrew was bound to a cross and compelled to preach until he died of exhaustion; Jude was shot through with arrows; Matthias was stoned and beheaded; Stephen was stoned; Paul was beheaded in Rome; John died in exile. But the worst opposition and suffering was endured by Jesus Christ, the Son of God, who was spat upon, scourged, crowned with thorns, nailed to the cross, and pierced with a spear—and all for your sins and mine!

Dare we talk about persecution?

IV. God's Provision for Victory Over the Enemy

I JOHN 3:8. "For this purpose the Son of God was manifested, that he might destroy the works of the devil."

Christ is not only the Saviour of lost sinners and the remedy for their sin but He is also the source of power for the Christian to have victory over the enemy. "Who hath delivered us from the power of darkness [Satan's kingdom], and hath translated us into the kingdom of his dear Son" (Col. 1:13). All that detracts from the glory of God, such as pride, unbelief, fleshly lusts, despair—are all the works of the devil, and it was to destroy these that Christ came.

I JOHN 4:4. "Ye are of God, little children, and have overcome them [Satan's helpers]: because greater is he that is in you, than he that is in the world."

God is not just beside us to help us, He is *in* us! Satan is mighty, but Christ is *almighty!*

The story is told of a swan that was walking on the edge of the pond when a fox came slinking out of the bushes to devour him. In a flash, the swan took to the water. But the fox followed, swimming with strong strokes. The swan, instead of trying to swim away, turned suddenly and came at the fox, grabbed his ear, and pulled his head down under the water, and the fox drowned!

The swan was weak on land, but he could win the attack when he was in his natural environment—in his element. We, too, are weak in our flesh, but strong in the Lord; in Him the Christian is in his spiritual element! "Resist the devil, and he will flee from you."

V. Our Part in Victory Over the Enemy

A. VICTORY COMES THROUGH FAITH

I JOHN 5:4. "For whatsoever is born of God overcometh the world: and this is the victory that overcometh the world, even our faith."

"Whatsoever is born of God" is the new nature that God gave us at salvation. The faith is that which He gave us, too. "For by grace are ye saved through faith; and that not of yourselves: it is the gift of God: not of works, lest any man should boast" (Eph. 2:8-9). This new nature desires

The great enemy overcome by the GREATEST ONE working in the little ones

victory, and so the enemy is overcome by the "little children," because of the Great One Who indwells them and has given them a new nature! They can break loose from the net that has been flung over them!

Saving faith, remember, is more than just believing there is a God. Saving faith is the personal receiving of Christ, who saves those who believe to the extent of receiving Him. "Be it known unto you therefore, men and brethren, that through this man [Christ] is preached unto you the forgiveness of sins; and by him all that believe are justified from all things" (Acts 13:38-39).

The indwelling Holy Spirit is able and willing to wean us from the pattern and principles that we followed when we were under the power of Satan. Worldliness is a mark of spiritual immaturity. Just as a child wants "now" what he wants, so the worldling wants "now" what he wants regardless of whether it is good or bad or the will of God or not. Faith defeats the pull to follow the world; by faith we determine to follow Christ. "For we wrestle not against flesh and blood, but against . . . the rulers of the darkness of this world" (Eph. 6:12). The Lord Jesus, speaking of

His disciples, said, "They are not of the world, even as I am not of the world" (John 17:14). We are not of the world even though we have to live in it. The submarine is in the sea, but alas if the sea gets into the sub! One compromise with the enemy is sin. One drop of deadly poison is as deadly as a barrelful!

A pastor once said to a worldly member of his church, "I understand that you attend the theater."

"Oh, I don't go often," the man replied. "I only go for a treat once in a while!"

One might as well say, I don't eat out of the garbage can often, I just do so once in a while for a treat!

During the war days, our two small boys would watch for the moment when the guards of the concentration camp where we were interned would empty their garbage. Then the youngsters would scramble to see if there was anything we could eat. Discarded sweet potatoes, stems of native spinach, or turnip tops were all greatly prized. These we chopped up to give volume for our dinner of spinach water.

I remember how heartbroken we were when the guards

dumped cow manure on top of the garbage! But even that could be washed off, and we were glad for the extra food in our starvation days! Today, however, we do not eat from the garbage cans!

Oh, there might be some good food in the garbage, but if we have a bountiful table of good things and a refrigerator full of nourishment, we do not need to pick through garbage cans! But yet some Christians, to whom have been given all the riches of the good things in Christ, still scavenge for their entertainment from the muck of Hollywood. To all such God says, "Know ye not that the friendship of the world is enmity with God" (James 4:4)? And He calls on all such to humble themselves and submit themselves to God. He also says, "Resist the devil, and he will flee from you" (James 4:7).

I JOHN 5:5. "Who is he that overcometh the world, but he that believeth that Jesus is the Son of God?"

The world offers temporary enjoyment, but God offers eternal joy. Worldliness is a tyranny of the present over the eternal. To determine whether you are under such tyranny, ask yourself the following questions.

1. Do I care more for the conveniences and comforts of life than the will of God?
2. Do I chafe under inconvenient circumstances which God allows?
3. Do I envy those who have more than I do?
4. Do I seek out persons because of their position or possessions?
5. Do I jump eagerly at the prospect of some earthly pleasure, and drag my heels when it comes to spiritual things?

If your answer to these questions is yes, then you have not yet tasted victory over the world!

I JOHN 5:6. "This is he that came by water and blood, even Jesus Christ."

The blood refers to Christ's sacrifice on Calvary, which is the only remedy for sin. "Unto him that loved us, and washed us from our sins in his own blood" (Rev. 1:5).

The water refers to the Word of God and the Spirit of God. "Christ . . . loved the church, and gave himself for it; that he might sanctify and cleanse it with the washing of water by the word" (Eph. 5:25-26). Jesus said, "If any man thirst, let him come unto me, and drink. . . . But this spake he of the Spirit, which they that believe on him should receive" (John 7:37, 39).

Both water and blood came forth when the spear was thrust into the Lord's side on the cross.

I JOHN 5:7. "There are three that bear record in heaven, the Father, the Word, and the Holy Ghost: and these three are one."

This verse is not included in the most authenic manuscripts but seems to have been inserted by copyists and translators at a later date.

There are very few such unsubstantiated verses in our English Bible, and this need not shake our faith in the trustworthiness of the English translation.

Have you wondered just how we know that our New Testament is dependable? True, the original manuscripts are no longer available; but there is even now in a museum a manuscript, transcribed about 250 A.D., which is only one step from the originals. Another interesting fact is that there are writings from Christians of the second and third centuries which are available today, and which quote at great length from the New Testament until almost every verse of our present Scriptures is included. One writer speaks of knowing the Apostle John personally. How close this brings us to John himself!

I JOHN 5:8. "And there are three that bear witness in earth, the Spirit, and the water, and the blood: and these three agree in one."

The Spirit of God, the Word of God, and the blood of Christ stand unitedly as the answer for salvation, and victory over Satan. We overcome by the Holy Spirit indwelling us, the Word of God governing our minds, and the blood of Christ continually cleansing from all sin.

THESE THREE AGREE IN ONE →

The Spirit is the Spirit of Christ
The water is the Word of Christ
The blood is the sacrifice of Christ

THE SPIRIT

WATER

B. VICTORY COMES THROUGH THE WORD OF GOD

I JOHN 2:14. "I have written unto you, young men, because ye are strong, and the word of God abideth in you, and ye have overcome the wicked one."

Only as we feed upon the Word do we become strong warriors for the Lord. The Word of God is our weapon for spiritual warfare. Christians are told to take "the sword of the spirit, which is the word of God" (Eph. 6:17). "The word of God is quick [living], and powerful, and sharper than any twoedged sword" (Heb. 4:12). This weapon must be used; it is no mere ornament to gather dust on the table.

Here God challenges the young men, those who are strongly decided for Christ and in the prime of Christian experience. And to the Colossian believers the Apostle Paul wrote, "Beware lest any man spoil you [defeat, and strip you of victory] through philosophy and vain deceit, after the tradition of men, and after the rudiments of the world, and not after Christ" (Col. 2:8). The opinions of the philosophers of this world are based upon rationalism and traditionalism, and not on the word of truth, and "Both he that helpeth shall fall, and he that is holpen shall fall down, and they shall all fail together" (Isa. 31:3).

C. Victory Comes Through Being on Guard

I John 3:7. "Let no man deceive you."

People today, like those in Bible days whom God accuses, are easily duped into thinking what they want to think. "The prophets prophesy lies in my name: I sent them not, neither have I commanded them, neither spake unto them: they prophesy unto you. . . . a thing of nought, and the deceit of their heart" (Jer. 14:14). The master-deceiver can use as his messengers so-called ministers of the Gospel who offer sawdust instead of the bread of life. "For such are false apostles, deceitful workers, transforming themselves into the apostles of Christ. And no marvel; for Satan himself is transformed into an angel of light. Therefore it is no great thing if his ministers also be transformed as the ministers of righteousness" (II Cor. 11:13-15).

I JOHN 4:1. "Try the spirits whether they are of God."

To be godly does not mean you need to be gullible! Too many are mesmerized by oratory, or personality, or talent, and they have but little conviction. The Apostle Paul wanted the Colossian believers to "continue in the faith grounded and settled, and be not moved away from the hope of the gospel," which they had heard (Col. 1:22). For this reason he warned them lest any man should beguile them with enticing words (Col. 2:4).

Just because a man is a minister does not mean that he is right. What he preaches is to be tested by such biblical doctrines as: the Bible is infallible and verbally inspired; God is one God but three Persons; all men are lost sinners without Christ; salvation is by being born again by faith in Christ; saving faith produces holiness; there is a heaven and a hell, and no second chance after death; the saved are saved forever; the Lord is coming again for His Church, and so on.

When we accept the doctrines (or teachings) of the Bible, we rejoice the heart of God and make ourselves happy. "Thy word was unto me the joy and rejoicing of mine heart: for I am called by thy name, O Lord God of hosts" (Jer. 15:16).

D. Victory Comes by Cooperating with God

I John 5:18. "He that is begotten of God keepeth himself and that wicked one toucheth him not."

Do you really want to be kept? Victory is available if you are willing to be kept! Do you hate sin? Are you sure you are not harboring it secretly? Have you willingly and joyfully set yourself in opposition to Satan's temptations? Only God can do the keeping, but you must cooperate with God by wanting to be kept.

Crossing the street with my little boy one day, he kept tugging away. "I go by myself!" Suddenly he got away, and was off like a dart. But almost immediately he stubbed his toe and fell flat on his face! You know the rest of the story—tears, a bloody nose, self-pity! He just did not want to be kept! After that fall, though, he was glad to slip his hand in mine and walk along quietly. He had found it paid to be kept!

It is God's will that all believers be strong. Why, then, are there so many feeble saints? God offers His strength to us; it is up to us to accept and use His strength.

Also, we must determine we will make no compromise with the enemy. "Wherein in time past ye walked according to the course of this world, according to the prince of the power of the air [Satan], the spirit that now worketh in the children of disobedience" (Eph. 2:2).

A true story is told of a drummer boy who was captured during the Civil War. He was ordered to drum for his captors or face execution. With the courage of his convictions, he suddenly jumped up and stamped on his drum smashing it to pieces. "I can never use this drum for the enemy!" he shouted. He was executed.

Never should Christians work in harmony with those who are the enemies of the truth. "Now we command you, brethren, in the name of our Lord Jesus Christ, that ye withdraw yourselves from every brother that walketh disorderly, and not after the tradition which he received of us. . . . And if any man obey not our word by this epistle, note that man, and have no company with him, that he may be ashamed" (II Thess. 3:6, 14).

There can be no ecumenical unity in this age as far as God is concerned, for He warns against being unequally yoked together with unbelievers. Those who love the Lord and the truth can only unite with those of like mind in the Lord. "Now I beseech you, brethren, mark them which cause divisions and offences contrary to the doctrine which ye have learned; and avoid them" (Rom. 16:17). The doctrine in this verse refers to the Holy Scriptures and not to the traditions of any church.

"Finally, my brethren, be strong in the Lord, and in the power of his might. . . . take unto you the whole armour of God, that ye may be able to stand against the wiles of the devil. For we wrestle not against flesh and blood, but against principalities, against spiritual wickedness in high places. Wherefore take unto you the whole armour of God, that ye may be able to withstand in the evil day, and having done all, to stand" (Eph. 6:10, 13).

I JOHN 5:21. "Little children, keep yourselves from idols."

We do not keep ourselves. No! But we do want to be kept!

No man can have two masters. Either he will serve God and the truth, or the enemy. How Satan would like to get us back to worshiping him!

During the occupation of a small country by enemy forces, the nationals refused to bow to the conquerors although they did not dare to resist openly by violence. However, they did the only thing they could. When any soldiers of the occupation army entered a restaurant or any public place, the natives would silently get up, pay their bill, and leave. Their silent protest was very loud indeed!

Are we as loyal to our Lord and King? Or are we co-operating with the enemy to keep our popularity, or job, or friends? Would we thus deny our Lord? This is idolatry! To try to keep step with God and with His archenemy is idolatry.

Listen to what the Apostle Paul has to say on this subject: "We then as workers together with him, . . . giving no offense in any thing, that the ministry be not blamed: but in all things approving ourselves as the ministers of God, . . . by the word of truth, by the power of God, by the armour of righteousness on the right hand and on the left, . . . Be ye not unequally yoked together with unbelievers: for what fellowship hath righteousness with unrighteousness? and what communion hath light with darkness? and what concord hath Christ with Belial? And what agreement hath the temple of God with idols? for ye are the temple of the living God; . . . Wherefore come out from among them, and be ye separate, saith the Lord, and touch not the unclean thing; and I will receive you" (II Cor. 6:1, 3-4, 7, 14-17).

Those who try to serve two masters will find that they are not serving the Lord at all, and when trouble comes, He will say to them, "Go and cry unto the gods which ye have chosen; let them deliver you in the time of your tribulation" (Judges 10:14).

'Mid the storms of doubt and unbelief, we fear,
Stands a Book eternal that the saints hold dear;
Thro' the restless ages it remains the same.
'Tis the Book of God, and the Bible is its name!
    The Old Book and the Old Faith
    Are the Rock on which I stand!
    The Old Book and the Old Faith
    Are the bulwark of the land!
    Thro' storm and stress it stands the test,
    In ev'ry clime and nation blest;
    The Old Book and the Old Faith
    Are the hope of every land!

QUESTIONS

1. What was Satan's sin? Isaiah 14:12-14.
2. How do we know the serpent that tempted Eve was the devil? Revelation 12:9-10; 20:2.
3. Does Satan use men sometimes? Acts 13:8-12.
4. Who keeps men from believing? II Corinthians 4:4.
5. Is God tolerant of error? Galatians 1:8-9.
6. Who can give victory? I Corinthians 15:57.

7. How do we cooperate with God in being kept?
   II Corinthians 7:1.
8. What is another weapon against temptation? Mark
   14:38.
9. What is the one reason for remaining in contact with
   error? II Thessalonians 3:15.
10. What should we do about those who live in sin and
    error? Ephesians 5:11.

7

GOD'S TRUTH ABOUT
SALESMANSHIP

THE BELOVED APOSTLE JOHN was now an elderly prisoner on
the isle of Patmos. Many years had passed since the Lord
Jesus had returned to glory, and already the first century
A.D. was becoming a world of speculation and daring
thought. This world had its realists who insisted that Jesus
was but a man, and that Christianity was but one of the
religions of the century.

This is a pretty accurate description of our present day
as well. Some who call themselves Christian regard Christ
merely as a beautiful dream of man's spirit, and present
him to the world as the peasant-saint of Galilee. They try
to bring religion up to date by pulling the Word of God
apart and putting it back together again in what they consider improved form!

But the revelation from God ends with John, who was the
last of the inspired writer by God. The Book of books is
ended, finished, completed, filled full. We have all we need
to know and all God wants us to know in order to be saved
and to live as God wants us to live, and it is all written
down in "the holy scriptures, which are able to make thee
wise unto salvation through faith which is in Christ Jesus.
All scripture [the written Word of God] is given by inspiration of God, and is profitable" (II Tim. 3:15-16). No need
now for councils to gather to revamp doctrines, nor for

denominations to rethink truth, nor for men to have visions and trances to gain new messages from God.

Christ and His coming, His living and dying, His resurrection and ascension were historical facts; and these John tries to prove to skeptics and agnostics by telling of his own personal contact and acquaintance with Him. John said he saw and heard and handled this One Who had actually been right with him. He uses the personal terms, "We have seen and heard, . . . our hands have handled . . ."

There will always be those who deny and doubt, and John did not want to leave any loopholes for such. He writes his strong evidence to disarm the credulous, even as Peter asserted, "We have not followed cunningly devised fables, when we made known unto you the power and coming of our Lord Jesus Christ, but were eyewitnesses of his majesty" (II Peter 1:16).

There are no apostles such as "the twelve" today, nor eyewitnesses of the resurrected Christ. There is no need for special men through whom God will inspire more scripture, for now we have the New Testament to speak for God, and with these inspired books the message from God is complete.

There is no scriptural authority for any claims of "apostolic succession." Instead, every believer is a priest unto God, as indicated by I Peter 2:5: "Ye also, as lively [living] stones, are built up a spiritual house, an holy priesthood, to offer up spiritual sacrifices, acceptable to God by Jesus Christ." The spiritual sacrifices a believer offers up are: his own living body, his praises, his gifts, and his prayers (see Romans 12:1-2; Heb. 13:15-16; I Tim. 2:1).

Every believer in Christ should confess Christ with his lips (Rom. 10:9-10) and should feel a responsibility to witness for Christ. Christ told His apostles, "Ye shall be witnesses unto me" (Acts 1:8). Not everyone can be a missionary in the sense of going to a foreign land, but everyone can be a witness for Christ, if only his heart is filled with a love and compassion for the lost which constrain him to tell what Christ has done for him (II Cor 5:14).

The Apostle Paul spoke of himself and his coworkers as ambassadors for Christ. An ambassador of a monarchy represents his king in a foreign land. Earth is the foreign land to which our King, now in heaven, has sent us as ambassadors. An ambassador must be in good standing with

THE SPIRITUAL MAN

his government; he must be utterly loyal to his king and speak for him. The ambassador, we might say, is a salesman for God.

The believer represents his King with God's message of reconciliation: "Now then we are ambassadors for Christ, as though God did beseech you by us: we pray you in Christ's stead, be ye reconciled to God" (II Cor. 5:20).

I. The Product We Offer As Salesmen for God

I JOHN 1:1. "That which was from the beginning."

The beginning before the world, the beginning of creation, the beginning of the Gospel message, and the beginning even of the Word of God, before all these Christ was the Source of the works of God which lie out of sight in eternity past. There is no beginning when Christ was not the Creator. This is the One John says that he had heard and seen and handled. This could not refer to God the Father, nor God the Holy Spirit, for "God is Spirit," and "no man hath seen God at any time," for God does not have physical form. But God the Son did take a human body: "God was manifest in the flesh . . . preached unto the Gentiles, believed on in the world, received up into glory" (I Tim. 3:16). This is the One John is offering to the sin-sick world: Jesus the Saviour!

Christ must be seen, as it were, through a two-dimensional viewer to make Him stand out in bold relief as God-man. Leave out one part of His nature, and you have a flat, unfinished picture.

I JOHN 1:2. "That eternal life, which was with the Father, and was manifested unto us."

Try to imagine the meaning of "eternal." You can't do it! Man can explain nothing that does not lie within the

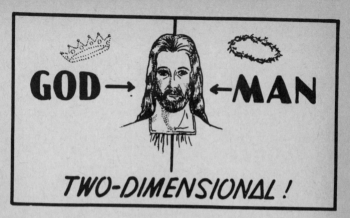

scope of his limited experience. Apart from Christ and His word, we could never know of eternity.

I JOHN 1:1-2. "The word of life, for the life was manifested . . . that eternal life."

Jesus said, "I am the resurrection, and the life: he that believeth in me, though he were dead, yet shall he live: and whosoever liveth and believeth in me shall never die" (John 11:25-26).

For the believer, one who believes in Christ as his Saviour from hell and the sting of death, the "valley of the shadow of death" is indeed only a valley and a shadow, and not a dead end! Hallelujah! Physical death is simply release from this sad old earth and a step into glory; We do not even go through the valley alone. We can say, "Thou art with me." Not only do we have Him *with* us but he is *in* us and we are in Him! Believest thou this? We walk as children of God in step with our Lord here, and keep right on walking right through the valley of death, and right on to our heavenly home!

DEATH VALLEY

DEATH IS NOT A DEAD END!

People have said to me, "If someone came back from the dead and told us what happened, then I would believe."

Well, some have come back from the dead: Jesus Christ and the Apostle Paul; Paul was not permitted to give a complete account of all he saw and heard, but one thing he was able to pass on to us, and that was that when the believer dies he goes immediately to be with the Lord (II Cor. 5:1-8). And that is far better than the best that life on earth can offer. No wonder Paul was homesick for heaven! He said, "For me to live is Christ; and to die is gain" (Phil. 1:21).

Life for the dead! This is our message for a dying world. "Though he were dead, yet shall he live." Men and women who are "dead in trespasses and sins," and walking and talking spiritual corpses with only the grave and eternal hell ahead of them, may have life if they will only receive and believe Christ. "Life begins when Jesus comes in."

If there were ever needy customers the people of this world are. And if ever any salesman had a worthwhile *product* to offer, we Christians do. As old age creeps on, the believer may grow feeble physically, but his future grows brighter as it comes closer. "For which cause we faint not; but though our outward man perish, yet the inward man is renewed day by day. For our light affliction, which is but for a moment, worketh for us a far more exceeding and eternal weight of glory; while we look not at the things which are seen, but at the things which are not seen: for the things which are seen are temporal; but the things which are not seen are eternal" (II Cor. 4:16-18)

No wonder John is sold on his product—the glorious living Lord!

So now, instead of using the impersonal terms, suppose we substitute the name of Christ to Whom they refer as we read the words, "Christ, who was from the beginning, . . . Christ was manifested, and we have seen Him." He is *life* for the sin-deadened: *bread* for the soul-hungry: *light* for the sin-blinded: *truth* for the seeker. This is the product that we are to "sell" to the world "without money and without price" (Isa. 55:1). This salesmanship should be easy, for the product is free!

One can't help but wonder though, why in the name of reason do people put up such sales-resistance against God! It is almost as if they were afraid He were trying to rob them of their money or their life!

Each day apart from God, the lost sinner is building, brick by brick, a prison tower around himself. The wall is thick and high. And it seems impossible to get our message through to him. Impossible? Yes, impossible for us. But "with God all things are possible," for there is always the skylight overhead through which the message may shine. To such as these God sends us as representatives of Christ, and to those who thus serve Him He says, "I the LORD have called thee in righteousness, and will hold thine hand, and will keep thee, and give thee for a covenant of the people, for a light of the Gentiles; to open the blind eyes, to bring

SELF-MADE
PRISON OF SIN

out the prisoners from the prison, and them that sit in darkness out of the prison house" (Isa. 42:6-7).

On returning from active service on the mission field in
poor health, I wondered what to do to occupy my time and
help supplement our income. I answered an ad in the paper
for salesladies to sell silverware from house to house. So I
learned the procedure and the sales speech, and was sup-
plied with samples and a list of prospective customers. I
set out in high hopes.

As I sat across from unhappy people, and saw their sin-
sick faces, I knew that I could never be content to sell
silverware. What they needed was the Lord.

I found myself giving my testimony, and talking about
Him and not the silver!

Result? No sales of silverware, but a convert for the Lord!

I turned in my sample case, saying, "There is only one
product I can sell, and that is the Lord Jesus Christ, the
Saviour for those who will receive Him."

What a product we have! And we need not be embarrassed when we present our product, we need not apologize
for being a salesman!

II. The Preparation for Salesmanship for God

I JOHN 1:1. "That which we have heard."

John was not going by hearsay. He had actually heard the Lord's voice during the years he accompanied Christ in His public ministry. Today, however, we do not have this privilege of hearing Jesus with our physical ears. Instead we hear Him through the written Word. This is nonetheless the voice of God.

God's message cannot be received and believed unless it is heard. "Faith cometh by hearing, and hearing by the word of God" (Rom. 10:17). Because faith comes by hearing the Word of God, the devil seeks to prevent people from hearing the Word or—if they have heard it—to steal it away from their hearts. "Then cometh the devil, and taketh away the word out of their hearts, lest they should believe and be saved" (Luke 8:12). The devil is also active in blinding the minds of them which believe not, "lest the light of the glorious gospel of Christ, who is the image of God, should shine unto them" (II Cor. 4:4).

Because the unsaved person cannot understand the things of God, the Bible is foolishness to him. It is pathetic to hear people discuss their opinions about spiritual things when their every word shows their ignorance of the truth. Of them God says, "For the preaching of the cross is to them that perish foolishness; but unto us which are saved it is the power of God. . . . hath not God made foolish the wisdom of this world? . . . it pleased God by the foolishness of preaching to save them that believe . . . But God hath chosen the foolish things of the world to confound the wise" (I Cor. 1:18-21, 27).

It is so common to hear unsaved people say, "I think it is this way. . . ." But it really does not matter a bit what they think, or I think, or anybody else thinks: the only thing that matters is what God thinks.

Sometimes men decide what they will believe because it sounds logical, or because it pleases them, or because their grandma told them so; but so few really know what God says. To be a salesman for God, we must *hear* His word.

I JOHN 1:1. "Which we have seen with our eyes."

Now comes the act of looking by faith to "the Lamb of God, which taketh away the sins of the world" (John 1:29).

Think back to the time of Moses, when the people of Israel murmured against God. To rebuke them God sent poisonous serpents into the camp, and the malcontents were dying from the serpent bites. Then they called upon Moses to pray for them. God heard his prayer, and directed him to place a brass replica of a serpent high on a pole in the center of the camp. The people who were dying were told that if they would only look at the brazen serpent they would live. Now, just what magical powers did that brazen serpent have? None whatsoever! The faith of these people in God's promise brought them healing. God told them to look, and they looked, and so they were healed.

The Bible explains itself, and John 3:14-15 shows the deeper meaning of which the healing in the camp was merely the type. The whole world has been bitten by the serpent of sin and is sick unto death spiritually. Jesus Christ was lifted up on the cross of Calvary as the remedy for this soul-sickness, and God commands men everywhere, "Look, and live!" "As Moses lifted up the serpent in the wilderness, even so must the Son of man be lifted up: that whosoever believeth in him should not perish, but have eternal life."

This is the look that saves: the look of faith. The look of faith represents the moment that we come to Christ and receive Him as our Saviour. This is the beginning step of salvation, and of consequent salesmanship for God. No one can tell others about the life-giving Saviour until he himself has received life.

I JOHN 1:1. "Which we have looked upon."

Here is a different meaning from the look of faith for salvation. This has the deeper meaning of intense gazing,

adoration, and contemplation; being occupied with the
Lord in worship. Just as the spotlight follows the per-
former on the stage, so our very life is to be focused upon
this eternal Word of Life, our glorious Christ.

It is not enough to take the initial step into salvation by
asking Christ to save us, and to receive the gift of God,
eternal life. A lifetime of love and obedience should follow.
Such worshipful adoration and gazing upon the Lord as
we read the Word and pray is another requirement for
successful salesmanship. It is this that will change us into
His likeness. "But we all, with open face beholding as in a
glass the glory of the Lord, are changed into the same
image from glory to glory, even as by the Spirit of the
Lord" (II Cor. 3:18). "From glory to glory" has the meaning of "from one step to another in glorious spiritual
growth." When we cross a brook by stepping-stones, each
stone is another experience, another victory, and brings us
one step closer to the other side. So, as we gaze upon the
Lord by reading His Word, listening to His voice, and
meditating on His truth, our soul becomes saturated with

Him and His will, and we grow in grace and are better prepared for powerful salesmanship.

It takes time to grow, and time is something many people think they have too little of to spend it in reading and prayer. They are the losers in the long run, however. It takes time to gaze into the face of God. It takes time for your heart to become quiet before Him so that He can speak to you. If you are too busy for this, then you are too busy indeed. Better cut something out!

One lady told me she did not have time to read and study her Bible. I suggested that she take time early in the morning before the family was awake, but she said she was too sleepy then. "Why so sleepy?" I asked. She answered matter-of-factly, "We stay up so late watching the late television show."

It is only from the secret place of fellowship that we can go forth to "sell" to others "Him whom our soul loveth."

How John must have loved Jesus! No wonder he was called the "beloved disciple," and the "disciple whom Jesus loved"! And just why did Christ especially love John? No doubt because John loved Him especially. Jesus said, "If a man love me, he will keep my words: and my Father will love him" (John 14:23).

Years later, when John was a weary old man in exile, he was given the view of his Lord which is recorded in the book of Revelation, the book of "the unveiling" of Jesus Christ. Amid the visions of God's wrath upon guilty sinners, and the worship and praise of heaven, John saw the beloved face of the glorified Christ. How his heart must have been encouraged!

Did you ever have a favorite teacher in grade school? I did. As a lonely little girl in missionary boarding school in China and far from mother for many years, that teacher stood for all my empty heart loved. I adored her from afar, and watched her constantly. I copied her handwriting and mannerisms. I even acted up naughtily to gain her attention! She was the one bright spot in my life. I wanted to be like her!

Friend, do you love your Saviour as much as your family and friends? Well, you shouldn't! You should love Him exceedingly more—with all your heart and strength and mind.

I JOHN 1:1. "Which . . . our hands have handled."

At the Last Supper it was John who leaned upon the bosom of Jesus. Of course we cannot touch the physical person of Jesus as the disciples did, but we can lift to Him the hands of faith and accept His grace and love and salvation, and lay hold on eternal life (I Tim. 6:12).

We have spoken of the ears of faith—hearing unto salvation, the look of faith— believing unto salvation, the gazing of faith—growing in salvation, and now we come to the hands of faith—accepting salvation and passing it on to others. Now that we have heard, and seen, and looked upon, and received Him, now we are ready to break the living

Bread of Life and pass it to others. For your hands to be worthy to break the Bread, your heart must continually feast upon Him.

III. The Procedure for Salesmanship for God

I JOHN 1:2. "For the life [Christ] was manifested, and we have seen it, and bear witness, and shew unto you that eternal life."

This verse gives simple instruction on "how to do it." John gives no special pattern, no clever words, no sure-fire sales speech, but he puts his instruction in a nutshell: "We have seen it [Him], and bear witness, and shew unto you. . . ."

Once we have seen the Lord and love Him, then we simply pass on what He has done for us and what we have learned. We do not need to wait until we have a degree in theology, or until we have mastered rhetoric and logic. To bear witness is to tell just what we do know. The newest convert can begin to witness for the Lord the moment he is saved. The moment we are "sold" is the time to begin "selling," and even a new babe in Christ can be filled with the Spirit as he spends time in God's presence.

A normal Christian is not a hermit. God's command is not to hibernate, but to radiate! Hibernation does not guarantee holiness. Those who try to isolate themselves from the temptations of the world by entering a cloister, find that the world even follows them there, for they can't get away from themselves.

As Christ said, "My meat is to do the will of him that sent me, and to finish his work." On another occasion, he asked, "Wist ye not that I must be about my Father's business?" Just what was His business? He stated it in these words: "The Son of man is come to seek and to save that which was lost" (Luke 19:10).

Seeking the lost is to be our business, too. God does not take us to heaven the moment we are saved because He has work for us to do in reaching the lost for Him. He does not call the most talented perhaps to be His witnesses, but He does call those who are dedicated; and this is the one category into which all of us can fit.

"Behold, now is the accepted time; behold, now is the day of salvation" (II Cor. 6:2). These words are a warning not only for the lost but they are also a warning to Christians to get busy for God. It is now, or never; after death is too late.

I well remember standing at the bedside of a dying friend and hearing her say, "I had so many plans to witness to my family. I thought I had plenty of time. Now I have no strength, and I'm too weary to talk. How I pray someone else will reach them for me!"

Sad, sad! How many plans we have to be salesmen for our Lord! But we never quite get around to doing it!

I JOHN 4:14. "And we have seen and do testify that the Father sent the Son to be the Saviour of the world."

"To testify" is "to say so." The effectiveness of the missionary message lies not only in its words but in our love for the souls of others. When we *care* about them, then perhaps some of them will come to care about our Lord. We should all be "care packages."

For some amazing reason, God, in His grace, has chosen to use men and women to be His witnesses, and to speak through us the wonderful words of His love. Why didn't He choose angels to win the world instead of weak and faulty human beings? Well, angels have never been redeemed by the blood of Christ, so they do not understand salvation. They are curious, and would like to look into it all, but only the saved sinner can tell "that which he has seen and heard." We are called to be salesmen, or missionaries, the moment we are saved, and our first mission field is our own home and friends.

Then we are to extend our witness to our neighbors,

and to the ends of the earth. We are told to "go and tell."
If we can walk, we should walk for God. If we can talk, we
should talk for God. If we can be friendly then we can be
friendly for God! There is no place for "secret believers"
in God's plan. "If thou shalt confess with thy mouth the
Lord Jesus [Jesus as Lord], and shalt believe in thine heart
. . . thou shalt be saved. For with the heart man believeth
unto righteousness; and with the mouth confession is made
unto salvation" (Rom. 10:9-10). "Whom [Christ] we preach,
warning every man, and teaching every man in all wisdom;
that we may present every man perfect [mature] in Christ
Jesus" (Col. 1:28).

No souls are won to Christ without paying a price, and
the price will mean self-denial, persecution, hard labor, and
heartbreaking disappointments. Service that counts costs!
But one soul is worth everything! Your own soul was so
precious that Christ died to redeem you! And someone sac-
rificed time and energy to pray for you and witness to you.

To say that you love your family and never witness to
them is to lie. To say you love your friends, and never try
to lead them to Jesus, is a sad pretense of love. It is not

love to give expensive Christmas gifts and yet withhold the gift of God, the Saviour. It is not love to cook for and feed your family, and withhold the Bread of Life.

I JOHN 1:3. "That which we have seen and heard declare we unto you."

Witnessing for Christ is as simple as that. If you are saved, go tell somebody else of Jesus. "Go home to thy friends, and tell them how great things the Lord hath done for thee" (Mark 5:19). "That ye should shew forth the praises of him who hath called you out of darkness into his marvellous light" (I Peter 2:9). Since we are going to spend eternity in praising the Lord, why not begin practicing right now and praise Him to others? "Let your light so shine before men, that they may see your good works, and glorify your Father which is in heaven" (Matt. 5:16).

And yet, friends, it is possible to know all the doctrines, and be able to quote Scripture, and to have taken many courses in personal evangelism, and still not be winning souls to Christ. What is the trouble? Can it be that what is lacking has been the preparation of heart through time spent with God alone? Or is there a lack of love? Are we just professional Christian workers without the love of Christ constraining us? Perhaps the heart is cold, or backslidden and worldly?

We cannot live on yesterday's breath, or last year's sleep. So we cannot live a successful and fruitful Christian life on last week's blessing or last month's Bible study; there must be the lifeline between us and the Lord constantly.

Power in witnessing depends upon the power of God in our own heart. This power is provided by the indwelling Holy Spirit. "But ye shall receive power, after that the Holy Ghost is come upon you: and ye shall be witnesses unto me" (Acts 1:8). So said the Lord Jesus.

The measure in which Christians yield to the Spirit of God will determine the measure of power in salesmanship. God has not promised to empty a bucket of blessing on the head of some unfaithful Christian just because he wants to be a success in some special religious project! Power with God and power with men is not like a robe that we can put on at a moment's notice after it has been hanging in the closet gathering dust.

The faithful Christian is a link between God and the sinner, bringing the message of salvation to those who are lost. As ambassadors, witnesses, salesmen, missionaries— whatever we might call ourselves as we labor together with God, we need to be on the job day and night. Sad it is, that too often Christians are not "declaring" unto others the word of the Lord, and the link between God and the lost is missing. This is indeed the "missing link," if you please—the unfaithful salesman! Is this blank space a picture of you or me? God forbid!

When a new gold field was opened up, a party of experts sent in their reports on the new field, but somehow nobody seemed too impressed. One day, however, two young men

came to town with lumps of yellow ore in their pockets. "Where did you get it?" everyone asked.

"Oh, up there on the gold field. There's plenty more of it up our way."

Next morning every able-bodied man was off to the digging!

If we are going to "sell" others on our Lord, our lives must show the "nuggets." Let us say with the psalmist, "I have not hid thy righteousness within my heart; I have declared thy faithfulness and thy salvation: I have not concealed thy loving-kindness and thy truth from the great congregation" (Ps. 40:10).

IV. The Purpose of Salesmanship for God

I JOHN 1:3. "That which we have seen and heard declare we unto you, . . . truly our fellowship is with the Father, and with his Son Jesus Christ."

Why be a salesman for God? He has commanded us to witness, and that should be reason enough. Also, our love for souls constrains us to witness, and that should be reason

enough. But here is yet another reason: that others might
have fellowship with the Father and with the Son of God.

Until men come to God, the lost have no contact with
Him at all. They have no blessings except the good things
that come to all people who live on the earth. They have
no power in prayer. They have no hope beyond the grave.
God is not on their side, and they flounder on through life
with no hope and no God. They are in the clutches of the
devil and his demons, and will spend eternity with all un-
repentant evil men in the lake of fire.

How can we continue living in smug comfort and rejoicing in the security of God's love, and care nothing about
the lost around us?

On the other hand, what a joy it is to be in fellowship
with God, to be in His family and to know His approval!
To abide in Him, to love and obey Him, to love others to
Him—this is the sign that we are in fellowship with Him.
The believer's fellowship with God is based upon a mutual
love for Jesus Christ. The Father said, "This is my beloved
Son, in whom I am well pleased." The heart of the believer replies, "This is my beloved Saviour, in Whom I am
well pleased!"

After liberation from the concentration camps, our family still had a month-long ocean trip across the Pacific before
we would be safely back home. After the years of starvation
and the battle of Manila with all the shellings and bomb-
ings, it seemed to me that one more month on the high seas
with enemy submarines and air attacks was just one thing
too much!

But I shall never forget going out on deck early in the
morning after we had put out to sea. The shoreline of the
Philippines was fading behind us in the distance, and there
all around us were seventy-five navy vessels—all types and

sizes. We were right in the middle of a convoy! What a wonderful feeling! In convoy!

This is what the word "fellowship with the Father and with the Son" means to me, too. We are in convoy with God Himself! What need we fear? No wonder we are sure of reaching our destination! He will not drop us along the way. The triune God is convoying us to glory. This is the basis of our assurance and hope, and this is also one of our reasons for witnessing for Him: that others might come into the same convoy with us, that they also might have fellowship with God and with us.

I JOHN 1:3. "That ye also may have fellowship with us."

All believers are in the same convoy. We are given the responsibility of watching over each other even as God watches over us all and cares for us. We have been commanded, "Bear ye one another's burdens, and so fulfill the law of Christ" (Gal. 6:2). Fellowship with God includes harmony with His children. When one stumbles, all are affected; when one is glad, others rejoice with him; when one suffers, all should sympathize The sunshine of love shrivels up jealousy and selfishness just as the sun shrivels up garden slugs on a hot pavement. Christianity sanctifies friendship and makes it sweeter and more satisfying than it ever could be apart from God.

I JOHN 1:4. "And these things write we unto you, that your joy may be full."

How men and women are trying to find happiness in these days of turmoil! They travel the mad treadmill of life in fevered frenzy only to find emptiness.

God has promised us real joy. Not a joy based upon hilarity and activity and indulgence. Such joy often ends in debauchery, shame, and remorse. The joy of the Lord brings no sorrow with it, and the world cannot take it away, and circumstances cannot mar it.

Our joy will be full. Our joy is His joy! Jesus said, "These things have I spoken unto you, that my joy might remain in you, and that your joy might be full" (John 15:11). "I will see you again, and your heart shall rejoice, and your joy no man taketh from you" (John 16:22). His joy! When we are occupied with Him and His work, He is our joy!

But the salesman for God does not have to wait till glory for all his joy. It begins right here on earth. We have His joy available right now! Earthly happiness comes from happenings, but the joy of the Lord comes from knowing that we are right with God and that we are bringing others to know Him too. Christian joy grows as we grow in obedience and Christlikeness. The only thing that can rob us of this joy is sin.

A convert gave this testimony: "I had always tried to live a life full of pleasure before I was saved, and I looked on Christianity as a burden and a bore. But now that I know

Christ as my Saviour, I find that He is my pleasure. Instead of a bore, my life is a joy and a delight!"

"Your joy may be full!" The salesman for God will have joy when he wins others to Christ. John says, "I have no greater joy than to hear that my children walk in truth" (III John 4). Paul writes to his converts, "Therefore, my brethren dearly beloved and longed for, my joy and crown, so stand fast in the Lord" (Phil. 4:1). "For what is our hope, or joy, or crown of rejoicing? Are not even ye [the converts] in the presence of our Lord Jesus Christ at his coming? For ye are our glory and joy" (I Thess. 2:19-20).

Not only does the soul-winner experience great joy, but the converted sinner does, too. He rejoices in his salvation. A good illustration is Philip's Ethiopian convert, who "went on his way rejoicing" (Acts 8:39). "Now the God of hope fill you with all joy and peace in believing, that ye may abound in hope, through the power of the Holy Ghost" (Rom. 15:13).

But greatest joy of all is in heaven, where the angels and God Himself rejoice over every sinner that repents. The Good Shepherd has found the lost sheep! Jesus described

this joy in the parable of the shepherd seeking the one lost sheep: "And when he hath found it, he layeth it on his shoulders, rejoicing. And when he cometh home, he calleth together his friends and neighbours, saying unto them, Rejoice with me; for I have found my sheep which was lost." And then Jesus added, "I say unto you, that likewise joy shall be in heaven over *one* sinner that repenteth" (Luke 15:5-7).

Talk about real joy! And you may be filled with such joy! Besides this, it is wonderful to know that those who labor to witness to souls, and pluck them from the fire of the judgment of God will experience "exceeding joy" when Christ presents them before His Father's throne: "Now unto him that is able to keep you from falling, and to present you faultless before the presence of his glory with exceeding joy, to the only wise God our Saviour, be glory and majesty, dominion and power, both now and ever. Amen" (Jude 23-25).

I JOHN 5:21. "Little children, keep yourselves from idols."

With such a glorious product to offer to the world, how could any Christian even think of not loving and serving Him with all his strength and heart and mind? And yet, can it be that we let days go by without witnessing to anyone? Do we allow the fear of man, the fear of unpopularity, the fear of failure, the fear of hard work block our willingness to be salesmen for God? Usually our excuses are nothing more than selfishness, and selfishness is self-love, which is idolatry.

Do you remember Peter's steps downward to the moment of denying his Lord? They began slowly. To begin with, he had just a spirit of pride, and this came even after

Christ had warned him that he was going to be tempted by Satan (Luke 22:31-34).

Next, in the garden, Peter slept when he should have been watching and praying. Even yet his self-confidence was unshaken (Luke 22:39-46).

It was no wonder, then, that when the mob came to arrest Jesus, that Peter acted as he did. He was still self-confident, and as a result trusted his skill with the sword, instead of trusting Christ (Luke 22:49-51).

And so the steps go on down, down, down—following afar off and denying his Lord three times. Why was he such an easy prey? Selfish fear, self-importance, self-confidence, self-comfort, and self-defense! Doesn't this sound mighty like us so much of the time?

Thank God, Peter wept bitterly over his failures and his denial of his Lord (Luke 22:54-62). Later the Lord let Peter know He forgave him and would use him in His service.

What grace God has bestowed upon all of us, that we too may come back and confess our sins and forsake our unfaithfulness, and find mercy! Have we been selfish and unconcerned about the souls of the lost? Have we been careless and worldly? Have we cared more for ourselves than for the service of the Lord?

Oh, why go back to our own selfish ways and the pleasures and approval of the world when we have the Word of Life, the living God?

> Jesus, Thou Joy of loving hearts,
> Thou Fount of life, Thou Light of men!
> From the best bliss that earth imparts,
> We turn unfilled to Thee again.
>
> Thy truth unchanged hath ever stood;
> Thou savest those that on Thee call;
> To them that seek Thee, Thou art good,
> To them that find Thee, All in All!
>
> We taste Thee, O Thou Living Bread;
> And long to feast upon Thee still;
> We drink of Thee, the Fountain Head,
> And thirst our souls from Thee to fill.
>
> O Jesus, Thou dost ever stay;
> To make our moments calm and bright,
> Chase the dark night of sin away,
> Shed through our heart Thy holy light.

QUESTIONS

1. How did God give His Word? II Peter 1:21.
2. Was the word of the apostles only the word of men? I Thessalonians 2:13.
3. Who was the apostle called by the glorified Christ? Acts 9.
4. How many people actually saw the resurrected Christ? I Corinthians 15:6-8.

5. What is the soul-winner's message? II Corinthians 4:5;
   Acts 4:20.

6. What is God's promise to those who witness? Galatians
   6:9; I Corinthians 15:58.

7. What is the real source of our joy? Philippians 4:4;
   Psalm 16:11.

8. What is the result of looking unto God? Psalm 34:5.

9. Should Christians share interests with others? I Corinthians 12:26.

10. What makes the believer rejoice? II Corinthians 1:12,
    14.

8

GOD'S TRUTH ABOUT HOW WE CAN KNOW HIM

THE WORD "know" is used some 38 times in the book of First John. This is not a message of "maybe" or "I hope so." This message is as sure as the character of God Himself. God's Word is truth as well as eternal. "For ever, O LORD, thy word is settled in heaven. . . . The entrance of thy words giveth light; . . . Thy word is true from the beginning: and every one of thy righteous judgments endureth for ever" (Ps. 119:89, 130, 160).

Even though one does not have a higher education in secular things, he can still know God's Word, for the Lord speaks to the heart as well as to the mind. There are Christian workingmen and homemakers who know the reality of God's truth even better than some Christian university professors. Why? Perhaps because the uneducated take what God says by faith and at face value, while the educated Christian person is so often occupied in analyzing and outlining and dissecting and teaching God's Word that he has little time to meditate on it and apply it to his everyday life.

In the Epistle of John, God has given us at least seven sure truths in verses that contain the word "know."

1. We can *know* the need of a Saviour. I John 2:4, 11; 3:1, 6, 15; 4:6, 8; 5:19.

2. We can *know* the Saviour. I John 2:13, 14, 29; 3:5; 4:2, 7, 16; 5:20.

3. We can *know* obedience to Him. I John 2:3-5, 29; 5:2, 18.

4. We can *know* truth from error. I John 2:18-19; 4:2, 6.

5. We can *know* power in prayer. I John 5:14-15.

6. We can *know* the message to give others. I John 2:20-27; 3:14.

7. We can *know* salvation for sure. I John 3:2, 14, 19, 24; 4:13; 5:9-13, 19.

We will not attempt to cover all these in these pages, for they have already been touched upon in the preceding chapters of this book, but we will consider something on the subject of knowing God personally in *deliverance* (salvation), *dedication* (growth), *discernment* (knowing truth from error), *dependence* (eternal security).

WE CAN KNOW GOD PERSONALLY

Satan knows and believes about God, but he does not know Him as his God. The unsaved can know about God, but He is not their God. They may accept the good things of life and admit that they come from God; they may be grateful for them, but still not realize that God intends that His goodness should lead men to repentance (Rom. 2:4). They must come to repentance, and they must accept the Saviour before they can know God personally. "Ye shall seek me, and find me, when ye shall search for me with all your heart. And I will be found of you, saith the LORD" (Jer. 29:13-14).

I JOHN 3:6. "Whosoever sinneth [continues on in persistent sin] hath not seen him, neither knoweth him."

The ungodly might be "ever learning and never coming to the knowledge of the truth." Even as the Pharisees, who prided themselves in their religious knowledge and practice but knew not God and rejected Christ, so the unsaved person flounders in spiritual blindness.

BLIND LEADER OF THE BLIND

True, no one can know God fully and absolutely, for finite minds cannot fathom the infinite: only God can fully know God. But we can come to know Him as our God and personal Saviour and Friend.

I. Knowing God Begins with Deliverance (Salvation)

"And they that know thy name will put their trust in thee: for thou LORD, hast not forgotten them that seek thee" (Ps. 9:10).

To know God is to love and prize Him above all others. We should be able to say with the Apostle Paul, "I count all things but loss for the excellency of the knowledge of Christ Jesus my Lord" (Phil. 3:8). It is vitally important to know God personally, and to *know* that we know Him.

To know implies not only that we are informed about Him but that we know we have believed on Him and have trusted our soul's salvation to Him, and that we have fellowship and communion with Him. There must be the transaction of trust and faith, of receiving Christ—the moment

of decision. God gives us the contract of salvation, but we are to receive with open hand and heart.

I JOHN 5:20. "And we know that the Son of God is come, and hath given us an understanding, that we may know him that is true."

Christ entered into our guilt that we might enter into His glory! This promise is for those who have come to Him. Jesus said, in His high-priestly prayer, "This is life eternal, that they might know thee the only true God, and Jesus Christ, whom thou hast sent" (John 17:3).

I JOHN 2:13. "I write unto you, little children [new Christians], because ye have known the Father."

Small children know some things, but their knowledge is very limited. Likewise a new Christian knows some things.

For instance, he knows God is his Father, but he still has much to learn about the heavenly Father's character and power. The new Christian knows his sins are forgiven, but that is about all. Thank God! that is quite enough to begin with, but the babe in Christ should begin to grow.

II. Knowing God Includes Dedication (Growing Spiritually)

"But grow in grace, and in the knowledge of our Lord and Saviour Jesus Christ" (II Peter 3:18). This does not say that we grow *into* grace but that we grow *in* grace. We are to grow in spirituality and knowledge of the Lord which comes from communion and love and obedience. The better we know Him, the more we fall in love with Him.

However, as the new Christian makes progress in the Christian life, he will be conscious of his own weakness and be confronted by temptations. The babe in Christ is apt to be unwise, unfaithful, and even unloving at times. The tempter seeks to trip him up, and baits him with the things of the world, and at times he becomes discouraged. But at other times he is elated, so much so that he is apt to let down his guard.

A new Christian can be perfectly healthy and normal spiritually even when he is first "born from above." His food is the milk of the Word; his breath is prayer; his exercise is witnessing for God and living a holy life. The young Christian grows normally into spiritual maturity as he follows these requisites for spiritual health.

What a heartbreak it must have been for Paul to have to write to the Corinthian Christians, "And I, brethren, could not speak unto you as unto spiritual, but as unto carnal, even as unto babes in Christ. I have fed you with milk, and not with meat: for hitherto ye were not able to bear it, neither yet now are ye able. For ye are yet carnal" (I Cor. 3:1-3).

To be carnal is to walk after the flesh, to remain a babe in Christ, although a Christian for many years. These Christians to whom Paul wrote were weak and worldly believers, "fleshly" and self-centered and occupied with earthly things and people and ambitions instead of spiritual.

How sad it is to see Christians remaining in spiritual babyhood—giving the same testimony, quoting the same verses they always quote, praying the same phrases over and over again, and living the same undedicated life with the same worldly habits! They have not matured enough to know that there is anything more for them. They are selfish and sensitive, and keep the pastor busy visiting and soothing them! Either they are dispeptic and cranky from spiritual indigestion because they are not using the knowledge they have gained from the Word, or they are half starved because they are not eating normally. Between trying to spoon-feed some and "burp" others, the pastor is kept busy when he is not sticking pacifiers into the open, complaining mouths of quarreling and gossiping Christians. It's a wonder he gets any preaching done at all!

"For when for the time [the long time they had been Christians] ye ought to be teachers, ye have need that one teach you again which be the first principles of the oracles [revealed truths] of God; and are become such as have need of milk, and not of strong meat. For every one that useth milk is unskilful in the word of righteousness: for he is a babe. But strong meat belongeth to them that are of full age, even those who by reason of use have their senses exercised to discern both good and evil" (Heb. 5:12-14).

I JOHN 2:13. "I write unto you, fathers, because ye have known him that is from the beginning."

This term "fathers" has nothing to do with the self-claimed title of some religious leaders, for we are told not to call any man our spiritual father, "Call no man your father upon the earth: for one is your Father, which is in heaven" (Matt. 23:9).

The fathers here represent the mature spiritual Christian. These "fathers" know the Lord in a deeper and fuller way than new believers; the seeds of spring have developed into the rich fruit of autumn. As inward grace transforms the wrinkled face with the radiance of joy, so the grace of God radiates from the life of the mature Christian to light up the lives of those around. The "fathers" know the Word and doctrine, and know how to obey and use it. They know the Lord and His will for their lives. "All scripture is given by inspiration of God, and is profitable . . . for instruction in righteousness: that the man of God may be perfect [mature], throughly furnished [completely equipped] unto all good works" (II Tim. 3:16-17).

The normal Christian becomes more and more yielded to

God as he grows in grace. He is also weaned away from the baby-bottle need for signs and feelings and miracles. Instead, he is willing to believe God without any tangible demonstrations.

The normal Christian constantly walks and talks with the heavenly Father as a personal Friend; he doesn't pray only at stated times each day; he confesses sin as soon as it occurs and so knows unbroken fellowship. He knows how to wait upon the Lord in prayer. He knows how to discern truth from error. His life is fruitful in witnessing to others. Christian reader, are you a normal Christian?

However, even mature believers are not out of the reach of temptation by any means, and it seems that Satan works overtime to trip them up by anxieties and worry, by a cynical and critical spirit, or by covetousness and ambition. How important it is to call upon the Lord and to listen to His voice at just such times of testing as these!

To babes and advanced children of God alike comes the challenge of the Apostle Paul: "That I may know him, and the power of his resurrection, and the fellowship of his sufferings, being made conformable unto his death" (Phil. 3:10).

It is that last phrase that we stumble over: being made "conformable unto his death." This is the dividing line between the "little children" and the "fathers." Everyone desires to know the power of God, but few realize that power is a result of suffering and self-denial and subjection to God's will.

In each human heart is born the self or ego (the seat of our natural self-conscious being). This self was completely sold out to the devil until we were saved. Then we were born anew, and God gave us a new nature that is God-centered.

TAKING A BEATING!

SELF

SPIRIT

The Giant tries to mold things after his own ideas

Just as good and evil are opposites, and light and darkness, so are the new nature and the old nature (or the
flesh, or the self-life). The believer is sensitive to the presence of the Holy Spirit, and longs for victory over the old
ego.

Even saved sinners, as human beings, are prone to cater
to the old self, for the desire to build up oneself in the
opinions of others is natural. It is the ego that gives people
inferiority and superiority complexes and all the other
complexes as well! It is human for a person to want to
keep up with others, or to be better than others, or to have
what others have, and so feel hurt when he cannot. So
many personal problems stem from this giant self, the ego,
which will plague us right up to the gates of glory, and
we all know this only too well!

Some Christians in mental distress, instead of going to
the Word of God and claiming His victory, go to an unsaved psychiatrist or counselor who gives them unsaved ad-
vice from his own unsaved unhappy heart or from what
he has read from other unsaved and unhappy writers!

The main problem of Christians boils down to the conflict between the flesh (the self) and the spiritual nature: our acts against our conscience; our wants against the promised supply from God. In so much of our conflict, we turn our eyes away from the Lord and look at what we want and our environment instead of trusting Him.

Oh, Christians, let Christ be the very center of gravity of your whole life. He is not only *great,* He is the *greatest!* Instead of being intoxicated with self, let Him fill your horizon, and then you will not limp along spiritually but will be strong and vigorous for God.

It is possible for a believer to live in such a backslidden state that he acts like the unsaved. God grant that we may leave our groveling in the muck of self-centeredness!

Earth offers mere phantom and transient pleasures. Worldly indulgences, ambitions, and pleasures are all counterfeits of things that are real, and they are followed closely by anxiety, trouble, and problems. But when Christ is our life, we are "complete in him," and He is our remedy for sin day by day, and our complete satisfaction. He sought us, bought us, and brought us to Himself!

"If ye then be risen with Christ, seek those things which

are above, where Christ sitteth on the right hand of God.
Set your affection on things above, not on things on the
earth. For ye are dead, and your life is hid with Christ in
God. *Christ . . . our life*" (Col. 3:1-4) .

The believer is "hid with Christ in God" or, literally,
"bound up in the same bundle" with Christ in God. Is
Christ your very life? Are you interested in things mere-
ly pleasurable, or things spiritual and important? Which?
At conversion a Christian experiences a radical change;
Christ becomes the Christian's very life, his *ALL IN ALL*.

"For ye are dead" does not mean that Christians are dull
and dead personalities; just the opposite! They have new
life. As Christ died to deliver from sin, so He lives to give
power over sin. When He died, those who belong to Him
died too. As He rose from the dead, so believers in Him
were raised to live a new life with Him. He died *for* sin,
and they died *to* sin; thus they are no longer to live *in* sin.
The dead do not indulge! The *dead in sin* do not indulge
in the blessing of God, and the *dead to sin* do not indulge
in the enticements of Satan.

A dying man has little interest in earthly politics or lusts
or possessions.

How indelibly this was impressed upon us when we were
expecting to be killed by the enemy during the invasion of
the Philippines. Our few possessions in our little bamboo
hut and the vegetables we had worked so hard to raise all
faded into a mere shadow and the only thing that really
counted was that we would so soon seen the Lord face to
face. We gathered together as a family to make sure that
our small children really understood what it meant to accept Jesus as their own Saviour. We had done this with
them before, but this time we prayed with them again and
tried to prepare them for what might come. There was
little interest concerning personal ambitions, or physical

appearance, or degree of health—all these had faded into nothingness in the light of eternity.

Christian, are you really counting yourself dead to the things of sin, or are you still grasping at the straws of your old life apart from God? It is time to allow Him to produce some self-conviction and self-condemnation and self-crucifixion in your life instead of constant self-pity, self-excusing, self-exoneration and self-justification. "Ye that love the LORD, hate evil" (Ps. 97:10).

Since Christ is our life, then when He shall appear we shall appear with Him. He will be the Celebrity of all celebrities *in person!*

III. Knowing God Includes Discernment (Knowing Truth from Error)

I JOHN 2:20. "But ye have an unction from the Holy One, and ye know all things."

No one needs to tell the child of God what is right or wrong if he is really in fellowship with the Lord and in touch with the Word. The Holy Spirit is the "unction" or

If any man have not the Spirit of Christ, he is none of His.

HOLY SPIRIT

THE UNCTION takes place at salvation

anointing which we have from God at salvation. He is the anointing from the Anointed One—Christ. He gave this promise of the Holy Spirit to the apostles before He returned to heaven: "I will pray the Father, and he shall give you another Comforter, that he may abide with you for ever; even the Spirit of Truth; . . . he dwelleth with you, and shall be in you. I will not leave you comfortless: I will come unto you" (John 14:16-18).

When the believer is led by the Spirit of God, he does not need to listen to men's theories and speculations about heavenly things. Christ also told His followers, "I will send him [the Holy Spirit] unto you . . . when he the spirit of truth, is come, he will guide you into all truth" (John 16:7, 13). This is the same blessed Spirit who rested upon Christ Himself: "And the spirit of the LORD shall rest upon him, the spirit of wisdom and understanding, the spirit of counsel and might, the spirit of knowledge and of the fear of the LORD" (Isa. 11:2).

With such a teacher, even the uneducated may understand spiritual things! Certainly a Christian does not need to turn to unconverted philosophers to give him light, for they are walking in their own imaginations and will end up in outer darkness. "They obeyed not, nor inclined their ear, but walked every one in the imagination of their evil heart" (Jer. 11:8).

We can know the truth, and the truth will free us from depending upon humanism and from being deceived by Satan-inspired doctrines. Christianity is not building air castles or mansions of soap bubbles; Christianity is not conjecture and surmise. What God has revealed to man is all in black and white—the written scriptures.

Some think they must know all about all religions before they can know truth from error. How wrong this is! Know

the truth, and all errors will stick out like a sore thumb! No need to read pages of slander about a loved one before we can know if we love a good or bad person. We know what he is like just by knowing him!

I JOHN 2:21. "I have not written unto you because ye know not the truth, but because ye know it, and that no lie is of the truth."

The Christian's mind is enlightened to know the truth by the indwelling presence of God, his heart is sanctified by believing the truth, and his life is empowered as he obeys the truth. There is no shortcut to knowledge, but God does open the understanding of what we have learned by reading His Word and meditating on it.

In some people you see great evangelistic activity with little knowledge of the word; then again in others you see dead orthodoxy with sound doctrine but little knowledge of the Lord! It is possible to be sound in doctrine and active in evangelism, and yet have little time for loving God. There must be in the Christian a balance of truth, zeal, and love.

I JOHN 2:24. "Let that therefore abide in you which ye have
    heard from the beginning."

This does not refer to something that might have been
taught in some church or that someone has always believed; this is speaking of the truth which the inspired
writers had given to the believers from God, the message of
Him Who was from the beginning. This is the gospel of
the abiding presence of Christ: that the Holy Spirit indwells
the believer and is to feel completely at home in his life
and take full control. Can this be said of you, dear reader?
Is the holy God really "at home" in your heart and life—
at ease and comfortable? Are you completely satisfied in
Him? If not, then there is sin in your life.

I JOHN 2:24. "Let that therefore abide in you which ye have
    heard from the beginning. If that which ye have heard
    from the beginning shall remain in you, ye also shall
    continue in the Son, and in the Father."

The Christians to whom John wrote were exhorted to
stick to the teaching originally given them. If they did,
John said, they would continue living in fellowship with
the Father and the Son.

This passage is dealing with knowing the truth and abiding in harmony with God, and is not inferring that a
Christian can lose his salvation. Salvation is God's gift by
grace, and the Holy Spirit is the abiding seal, a guarantee
that we can never be lost again. The Apostle Paul, writing
to the Ephesian believers said, "Ye were sealed with that
Holy Spirit of promise" (Eph. 1:13). When were they
sealed? The first part of the verse tells us: after they trusted
in Christ subsequent to their hearing the word of truth,
the Gospel of their salvation. The seal indicates ownership.

We belong to God, and no one can pluck us out of His hand (John 10:28-29). He holds us securely and forever!

But this does challenge us to possess our possessions and to hold on to the truth we have received. God desires "that we henceforth be no more children, tossed to and fro, and carried about with every wind of doctrine, by the sleight of men, and cunning craftiness, whereby they lie in wait to deceive; but speaking the truth in love, may grow up unto him in all things, which is the head, even Christ" (Eph. 4:14-15). The Apostle Paul told the Colossian believers God's purpose: "To present you holy and unblameable and unreproveable in his sight: if ye continue in the faith grounded and settled, and be not moved away from the hope of the gospel, which ye have heard" (Col. 1:22-23).

I JOHN 2:27. "The anointing which ye have received of him abideth in you"

The Spirit of God never leaves us. He does abide. This anointing is not tongues of fire, or oil on the head, but the inward presence of God Himself. This is not a fitful emotion, not a capturing of excitement or rapturous ecstasy, but the serene presence of a holy Person who endues us with wisdom to discern truth from error.

All believers have received the gift of the Holy Spirit, and He is the Spirit of truth and error. He has never left the church, and there is no need to pray and emotionalize in order to receive this gift from God. He is already in us!

Remember, John wrote after 90 A.D. But in all his writings, inspired by God, he mentions nothing of signs and miracles and demonstrations and emotions to be given to believers. All such primitive demonstrations had long since ceased, and now the church depended only upon the written Word of God rather than upon gifts of healings and tongues. The gifts of the Spirit in our day are the gift of grace to bear suffering rather than healing, the gift of wisdom to know truth from error, the gift of faith to believe God without any special manifestation.

I JOHN 2:27. "And ye need not than any man teach you."

This does not infer that Christians cannot learn anything from other Christians. God has ordained pastors to preach and teachers to teach. "When he [Christ] ascended up on

high, he . . . gave gifts unto men. . . . And he gave some, apostles; and some, prophets: and some, evangelists; and some, pastors and teachers; for the perfecting of the saints, for the work of the ministry, for the edifying of the body of Christ" (Eph. 4:8, 11-12) .

To be taught by the Spirit does not mean that we become presumptuous and are unwilling to be taught by Spirit-filled men and women of God who have spent years in studying the Word, and have had years of experience teaching the Word. Such have been given to the church by God.

Believers taught by the Spirit do not need to accept any teachings which are not in harmony with the Word of God. The opinions and philosophies of men who do not know God are emptiness and vanity. In such cases, a Christian can say, "I have more understanding than all my teachers: for thy testimonies are my meditation" (Ps. 119:99) .

I remember so well a man coming to me after church one Sunday and saying, "You are doing evil in telling people to attend Sunday school and Bible classes. The Bible says we should not listen to anyone teaching us! I need none but God to teach me!"

"I agree that you need God to teach you," I replied. "In fact, what you have just said shows that you certainly need a lot more teaching!" I spent some time with him that day showing him how God has commanded men and women to teach others. Some of the Scriptures I used were: "These things teach and exhort" (I Tim. 6:2) . "Holding forth the word of life" (Phil. 2:16) . "Preach the word; be instant in season, out of season; reprove, rebuke, exhort with all longsuffering and doctrine" (II Tim. 4:2) . "And daily in the temple, and in every house, they ceased not to teach and preach Jesus Christ" (Acts 5:42)

I JOHN 2:27. "But as the same anointing teacheth you of
  all things, and is truth, and is no lie, and even as it
  hath taught you, ye shall abide in him."

The anointing is not an *it*. The anointing is a Person—
the Holy Spirit. Jesus, speaking of the Holy Spirit, called
Him the "Spirit of truth" (John 14:17). Jesus told His
disciples this about the ministry of the Spirit: "When he,
the Spirit of truth, is come, he will guide you into all truth"
(John 16:13). And as the Holy Spirit guides the believers
in Christ into all the truth, He teaches them to abide in
Christ.

This ministry of the Holy Spirit in revealing spiritual
truth to Christians is described by Paul the Apostle in this
way: "Eye hath not seen, nor ear heard, neither have entered
into the heart of man, the things which God hath prepared
for them that love him. But God hath revealed them unto
us by his Spirit: for the Spirit searcheth all things, yea, the
deep things of God. . . . Now we have received, not the
spirit of the world, but the spirit which is of God; that we
might know the things that are freely given to us of God.
Which things also we speak, not in the words which man's
wisdom teacheth, but which the Holy Ghost teacheth; comparing spiritual things with spiritual. But the natural man
[the man without God] receiveth not the things of the
Spirit of God: for they are foolishness unto him: neither
can he know them, because they are spiritually discerned"
(I Cor. 2:9-16).

IV. Knowing God Includes Dependence
(Eternal Security)

This matter of assurance of salvation, which springs from
complete dependence upon God to keep us to the end, is
one of the dividing lines between all truth and error. As-

surance of salvation ties in closely with the issue of salvation by faith alone, for the moment anyone intimates that a child of God can lose his spiritual sonship, or that a new creation in Christ can lose his new nature, he is guilty of error. The teaching that a child of God can lose his salvation is based on the error that salvation is earned by being good or holding out to the end, and heaven is gained by being faithful.

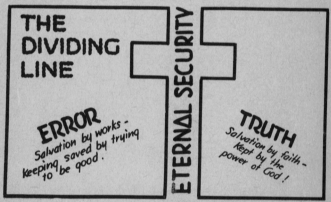

THE DIVIDING LINE

ETERNAL SECURITY

ERROR
Salvation by works - keeping saved by trying to be good.

TRUTH
Salvation by faith - kept by the power of God!

I JOHN 5:13. "These things have I written unto you that believe on the name of the Son of God; that ye may know that ye have eternal life, and that ye may believe on the name of the Son of God."

This entire book of First John is for the saved ones, the children of God, so this promise is for those who are in Christ. We may know for sure—not maybe—and not even "God willing," for God is willing. He said so! The whole purpose of this inspired writing is that we may *know*. To say we are saved is not presumption but simple belief in what God says. To refuse to believe what God says is to call Him a liar.

Scripture gives us no leeway for doubt. God has given us the witness and the written Word, and so each child of God can say, "I know whom I have believed, and am persuaded that he is able to keep that which I have committed unto him against that day" (II Tim. 1:12). When our earthly body dies, we continue to live with Him for all eternity. Hallelujah!

I was calling the attendance roll in one of my classes one morning, and I came to the name of one of the very faithful members who had died during the week. Without thinking, I called her name. There was silence. Then I remembered. Quietly, I answered for her, "Present, with the Lord!" It was a moving moment. How glorious to know for sure that those who belong to Him will always be with Him! The Lord Jesus, in His high-priestly prayer, prayed, "Father, I will that they also, whom thou hast given me, be with me where I am; that they may behold my glory, which thou hast given me" (John 17:24). Surely the prayer of Christ is not going to be denied!

I John 5:9. "If we receive the witness of men, the witness of God is greater."

So many of our everyday business transactions are based upon promises. The finance company loans and charge accounts are granted upon promises to pay. The bank promises to pay "on demand." Your check is a promise that you have money in the bank. We take the promises of men in dozens of ways every day, and every paper dollar bill is promise that the government has gold to back it up. But everyone knows that many, many people are unfaithful and fail to keep their promises. But God cannot fail; He cannot lie. God alone can be trusted. However, people often will trust lying men, and then doubt the holy God. The "witness" of God is His eternal Word, which is based upon His holy and eternal character.

I John 5:9. "For this is the witness of God which he hath testified of his Son."

God has testified concerning Christ in the Old Testament prophecies. All the Bible from cover to cover has one main theme—salvation—and one Hero, the Saviour. In the Old Testament alone there are some 333 fulfilled prophecies about Jesus Christ. God testified about Christ at His Baptism. We read in Matthew 3:17 about "a voice from heaven, saying, This is my beloved Son, in whom I am well pleased." In the first chapter of John's Gospel, John says that God told him, "Upon whom thou shalt see the Spirit descending, and remaining on him, the same is he which baptizeth with the Holy Ghost" (John 1:33). And John added, "And I saw, and bare record that this is the Son of God" (John 1:34). God gave further testimony concerning Christ in the New Testament through the apostles and prophets of the early church.

The Old Testament says, "Christ is coming!" The New Testament says, "Christ has come and is coming again!"

Peter, speaking to the Sanhedrin, boldly told them they had crucified "Jesus Christ of Nazareth, . . . whom God raised from the dead, . . . This is the stone which was set at nought of you builders, which is become the head of the corner. Neither is there salvation in any other: for there is none other name under heaven given among men, whereby we must be saved" (Acts 4:10-12).

I JOHN 5:10. "He that believeth on the Son of God hath the witness in himself."

When we have believed God's Word and received His Son, then we have the assurance within our hearts that we belong to Him. The believing comes before the witness. "The Spirit itself [Himself] beareth witness with our spirit, that we are the children of God" (Rom. 8:16).

A chrysalis could never understand or keep the laws that will be his life when it becomes a butterfly; it must be reborn first. It must enter that new existence before it can live the new life. So we cannot know God nor His will until we are born from above, and then we—like the chrysalis—experience a wonderful change. We know we live; our new manner of life proves it. We know we live because we have new desires and new interests and new practices that issue from the new nature born of God.

I JOHN 5:10. "He that believeth not God hath made him a liar; because he believeth not the record that God gave of his Son."

Why do some people refuse to believe? Perhaps because they do not want to be involved with righteousness. Perhaps they don't want to change their pattern of living. Some might think they have plenty of time to be religious when they are old.

Not too long ago, a young husband said to me, "I'm not ready to become a Christian yet. I don't want to settle down and live a dull life. I'm young, and I want to live a little."

He tried all that the world offered, and lived recklessly and foolishly, thinking he was having a good time. But today he is a broken man. He was smashed up in an auto accident while intoxicated, and his wife and child were killed. That young man has plenty of time now to think and grieve.

Others do not believe because they are too proud to admit that they need a Saviour. How dreadful it will be when they have to face Him as their Judge some day!

Some do not believe because they do not believe the message of salvation is true. They are calling God a liar, and trusting their own reason and warped intellect instead of the revealed Word of God.

Others say that they do believe, but they have never received Christ personally. They have not "believed unto salvation."

I JOHN 5:11. "And this is the record, that God hath given to
us eternal life, and this life is in his Son."

We have the record. God does not leave His message to
word of mouth; it has been written down so there can be no
mistake. "Thus saith the Lord!" is written throughout the
record—the Bible.

Salvation is by faith. And the person who has faith believes God even though there is no sign or feeling at all.
Some one says, "I feel I am saved. I've always felt that I
belonged to God." That is no proof! To begin with, none
of us has always belonged to God; all of us needed to be
born again. Besides, feelings change with the weather or
health and circumstances, and cannot be trusted. It matters not how we feel, or what we feel; assurance comes from
fact—what God and Christ have done, and what God has
promised!

Still others feel that their baptism and confirmation or
taking communion is helping to keep them saved. They
feel the church is their security as long as they are faithful
and pay their pledge and attend once in a while. Theirs is
a false security.

If you should ask me, "How do you know you are saved?"
I would answer, "How do I know I am *married*? Because
my husband and I have mutual friends? Or because we've
been together for thirty years? Or because we have community property? Indeed not! Those experiences do not
make us married! But I do know that I was present when
we were married, and I said 'I do,' and he said 'I do,' and
we received a marriage certificate. So it is with salvation.
I was there when it happened, and I know the day. I said
to the Lord, 'I do receive you,' and He said, 'Him that
cometh to me I will in no wise cast out. I do receive you!'

I have a certificate, too—the Word of God which says, 'He that hath the Son hath life.' "

Oh, yes, there have been feelings of joy and assurance that have followed that day of decision, but they are the *results* and not the *proof*. Thank God, our security does not depend upon our feelings or our faithfulness, but upon our dependence upon Him!

1 JOHN 5:12. "He that hath the Son hath life; and he that hath not the Son of God hath not life."

What a plain, clear statement—and in one-syllable words! Possessing Christ, we have life—God's life, spiritual life, abundant life. Our physical life is so temporal compared to spiritual life, which is eternal: "For what is your life? It is even a vapour, that appeareth for a little time, and then vanisheth away" (James 4:14)

But spiritual life includes everything for time and eternity. Christ is the Giver, and He is the Gift. This is not just an endless existence, but the soul's well-being forever. This is Christ's own life given to us—and not in limited measure. He says, "I am come that ye might have life, and that ye might have it more abundantly" (John 10:11).

In I John 5:12 we see two divisions of humanity—the haves and the have-nots! In which are you?

The sentence of death is already recorded against the Christ-rejecter, even though he is still physically alive. "He that believeth not is condemned already, because he hath not believed in the name of the only begotten Son of God" (John 3:18). "He that believeth not the Son shall not see life; but the wrath of God abideth on him" (John 3:36).

If you have received Christ, you have life! "He that believeth on the Son hath everlasting life" (John 3:36). This is God's promise. The security of the believer is dependency on God's keeping power, and not upon our holding-on power. Praise His name!

The sovereign God knows who are His—"those that are sanctified by God the Father, and preserved in Jesus Christ" (Jude 1). Just think! Set apart by the Father and preserved by Christ! No wonder we have assurance! We are not embalmed like a dead body and preserved in a glass case, neither are we preserved and pickled like relish on the pan-

PRESERVED ALIVE!

(NOT JUST PICKLED !)

try shelf. We are preserved *alive!* Assurance of salvation is not necessary for our safety, but it is needful for our satisfaction and for glorifying God.

Let me give you another illustration—which may be helpful. Suppose someone asked you, "How do you know your house belongs to you?" Would you say, "Well, I've lived in it for so long," or "My father lived here and I feel it is mine," or "I like it here, so it must be mine"?

None of these answers would hold up in court. Get out the deed! That's your proof!

I JOHN 5:19. "And we know that we are of God."

This statement leaves no loophole for doubt. But just in case you need further proof, here are some more verses from the Gospel of John: John 1:12; 3:16, 18, 36; 5:24; 6:39-40, 47; 10:9, 28-29; 14:1-3, 16; 17:3, 9, 11-12; 20:31.

And here are some verses from the epistles of Peter: I Peter 1:2-5, 18-21; 3:18; II Peter 1:1-3.

Again, here are some verses from the pen of the Apostle Paul: Rom. 3:24-28; 5:1, 9; 8:1, 28-39; Eph. 1:1-23; Phil. 1:6; I Thess. 1:4; II Tim. 1:9-12.

I JOHN 3:19. "And hereby we know that we are of the truth, and shall assure our hearts before him."

Because Christians perceive the love of God for them in laying down His life for them (I John 3:16), they respond to this love by loving God and by loving the brother who has need (v. 17). Christians who love in deed and truth and not merely in word (saying they love their brethren but doing nothing for them when they are in need) can say, "Hereby know we that we are of the truth and shall assure our hearts before him." One of the marks by which a

Christian can *know* that he is born of God is his love for God's children—"the brethren."

"Heart" is a term used so often in Scripture to designate the center of our being, our innermost feelings. The unsaved man has a conscience (or center of reason and being) that is untrustworthy because of sin. A "conscience seared with a hot iron" (I Tim. 4:2) is not a dependable guide. It is only when the heart is surrendered to the will of God that the conscience can be trusted at all.

I JOHN 3:20. "For if our heart condemn us, God is greater than our heart, and knoweth all things."

Certainly, when we face sin in our lives and let it remain unconfessed, the Lord also sees it. He is far more sensitive to sin than we are, and will have to rebuke and discipline His wayward child unless he confesses and forsakes it. He knows the secret sin we try to cover up, and He sees and discerns the motives behind our apparent good deeds. So if we look into our hearts and see insincerity and sin, and are convicted, how much more does God see? Be sure of this, you cannot hide your sin, and it must be dealt with—either by you in self-judgment, or by God in chastening.

I JOHN 3:21. "Beloved, if our heart condemn us not, then have we confidence toward God."

This verse was not written to the unsaved who have a disregard for God and a complacent spirit that leads them to say, "My heart doesn't condemn me!" And they go on in their sins.

This verse was written to people whom John addresses as "beloved." The beloved are the children of God, and they have confidence toward God because their hearts do not condemn them. The reason their hearts do not condemn them is their confidence that they were acquitted of

all charges of a holy God against them when they believed
in Christ as the One who died for their sins. They are
justified by faith (Rom. 5:1). God looks upon them through
the person of Christ, and sees them as they will be in eternity. His all-seeing eye sees them as He is going to make
them. And even though they are not yet perfect, He calls
them His beloved.

Oh, what grace! We are not merely subjects of the King
but we are the beloved children of the King. And as we
live in this world, we have confidence toward God because
our hearts condemn us not. We *know* we are saved. But
this certainty should not mean that we become careless or
that we will be unfaithful. We seek to please Him because
He loves us (we are His "beloved") and we love Him.

I JOHN 3:24. "And hereby we know that he abideth in us,
by the Spirit which he hath given to us."

The Holy Spirit (God Himself) indwells us forever!
How, then, could we ever be lost? The only way we could
lose our salvation would be to be taken out of the hand of
Almighty God, and for Him to be taken out of our heart.

This is an impossibility! To do this, the robber must be stronger than God! Jesus Christ said, "And I give unto them eternal life; and they shall never perish, neither shall any man pluck them out of my hand. My Father, which gave them me, is great than all; and no man is able to pluck them out of my Father's hand. I and my Father are one" (John 10:28-30). You see, even Satan cannot pluck the saint out of the Saviour's hand, and certainly we cannot take ourselves out of His hand, and neither will He let us fall through His fingers! With God the Spirit indwelling us, and God the Father and God the Son holding us, we have not just security, nor double security, we have three-fold security! Glory to God!

Neither shall any pluck them out of MY HAND.. or MY FATHER'S HAND

"Eternal" means eternal—not just a short time but forever. We have eternal life, which begins the moment we receive the eternal Son of God, and He will remain with us forever. This life is also called everlasting life. "For God so loved the world, that he gave his only begotten Son, that whosoever believeth in him should not perish, but have everlasting life" (John 3:16). In the Greek text of this verse, the word "have" is in the present tense, which expresses continuous action, and so we may say that one who believes on Christ "shall continue to have everlasting life." The verse means just what it says—one who believes in Christ will have life forever!

Some, when quoting the passage in II Peter 2:22, apply it to a Christian, maintaining he can lose his salvation. However, that whole chapter is speaking of those who know the truth and come to the knowledge of the Saviour, but have never been saved at all. We have people today— people who sample Christianity, even attend Bible classes and join a church, get baptized and live a moral life, but they do not believe, they have never been born again. When they turn away from the truth, then "it is happened unto them according to the true proverb, The dog is turned to his own vomit again; and the sow that was washed to her wallowing in the mire." God never speaks of His children as dogs and swine! We are the sheep of His pasture! It is impossible to lose something you never had. These false teachers never had salvation at all, so they didn't lose salvation.

Other favorite passages for presenting such an argument are Hebrews 6:4-9 and Hebrews 10:26-39. These passages refer to Jewish inquirers who came to the very brink of believing in Jesus as the Messiah and Saviour and then went back to the law of Moses and the sacrifices of Judaism. They had understood the message of the grace of God and had "sampled" the blessings of Christianity by meeting with the Christians in their fellowship meetings. These Jewish inquirers had even "gone along" with the miracles of the Holy Spirit so evident in apostolic times. They were like Simon the sorcerer (Acts 8:9-24), who followed along with the apostles and evidenced some belief and was baptized but never was saved. His believing was the kind James mentioned in James 2:19: "The devils also believe, and tremble." They were persuaded about the truth but did not believe unto salvation.

That these passages do not speak of a child of God losing his salvation is indicated by the words: "But *we* are not of them who draw back unto perdition; but of them that believe to the saving of the soul" (Heb. 10:39) and "But, *beloved,* we are persuaded better things of *you,* and things that accompany salvation, though we thus speak" (Heb. 6:9).

I JOHN 4:13. "Hereby know we that we dwell in him, and he in us, because he hath given us of his Spirit."

Here we are again directed to the fact of the indwelling Spirit of God! We *know* we are born again and children of God because the Spirit of God indwells us, but "if any man have not the Spirit of Christ, he is none of his" (Rom. 8:9).

The amazing thing is, that in spite of all the wealth of Scripture proving the keeping power of God, some people prefer to get their teeth into some verse that *might* sound

otherwise, and they worry that one verse to death trying to prove that God is a liar when He says the believer has eternal life and shall never perish. Why do people try to disprove such a wonderful truth?

I JOHN 3:2. "Beloved, now are we the sons of God, and it doth not yet appear what we shall be: but we know that, when he shall appear, we shall be like him; for we shall see him as he is."

This verse does not say that we shall see Him *if* we are faithful; and it does not say that we shall be like Him *if* we hold out to the end! It does teach we are the sons of God now, we shall be like Him, and we shall see Him. There are no qualifying requirements. Our becoming like Christ is all God's doing, all of grace, undeserved and unearned. "Even so, come, Lord Jesus!"

The world says, "While there's life, there's hope." God says, "Even after life, there is hope!" Christians have a hope to live by.

What comfort or peace could we have if our salvation depended upon our own faithfulness? Life would be full of fear lest we should be unable to "hold on" and "make it" to heaven, instead of being filled with the peace and confidence which is Christ's legacy to His own: "Peace I leave with you, my peace I give unto you: not as the world giveth, give I unto you. Let not your heart be troubled, neither let it be afraid" (John 14:27) . For the believer, this means release from guilt and dread and from fear and frustration. This is the peace that continues to multiply as we grow in our knowledge and consequently in our trust. "Grace and peace be multiplied unto you through the knowledge of God and of Jesus our Lord" (II Peter 1:2) .

God's tranquilizer is "the peace of God, which passeth all understanding" (Phil. 4:7) , which keeps the hearts and

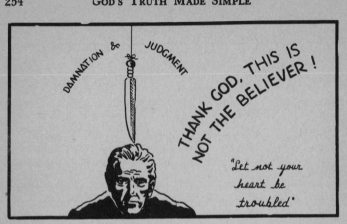

DAMNATION & JUDGMENT

THANK GOD, THIS IS NOT THE BELIEVER!

"Let not your heart be troubled"

minds who trust in Christ Jesus and present all their requests to Him. Faith in God is confidence in Him even
when He seems to act contrary to His promises, and appears
to be contradictory in His providence.

I JOHN 5:21. "Little children, keep yourselves from idols."

We are the temple of the living God. "What? know ye
not that your body is the temple of the Holy Ghost, which
is in you, which ye have of God, and ye are not your own?
For ye are bought with a price: therefore glorify God in
your body, and in your spirit, which are God's" (I Cor.
6:19-20).

God is a jealous God, and rightly so. His jealousy is not
sin, for He has the right to demand our worship. And when
you put self first in your life, you are worshiping self, and
this is idolatry. We are not to worship any other—not even
self. Self-confidence, self-interest, self-consciousness, self-oc-
cupation, self-will—all make a pretty impressive show of
spiritual idolatry!

Oh, we Christians would never make ourselves graven

images like the heathen do, but do we come close to worshiping *things* and our own *self*?

With all our modern enlightenment, are we so different from the heathen after all? We who know the living God, are we choosing to make unto ourselves gods that will demand nothing of us and cost us nothing? Are we bowing to our own image, our own will, our ego? Lucifer's sin was pride, and caused him to be cast out of God's presence. In his pride he wanted worship that belonged to God alone.

Christians, is this our sin? God forbid!

"His servants ye are . . . whom ye obey, . . . Now yield your members servants to righteousness unto holiness" (Rom. 6:16, 19).

> God calling yet! Shall I not hear?
> My sinful self shall I hold dear?*
> Shall life's swift passing years all fly,
> And still my soul in slumber lie?
>
> God calling yet! Shall I not rise?
> Can I His loving voice despise?

*Line changed by present author.

And basely His kind care repay?
He calls me still; can I delay?

God calling yet! And shall He knock,
And I my heart the closer lock?
He still is waiting to receive,
And shall I dare His Spirit grieve?

God calling yet! I cannot stay!
My heart I yield without delay!
Vain pride and sin, from thee I part;*
The voice of God has reached my heart!

QUESTIONS

1. Do the heathen know there is God? Romans 1:19-21, 28.
2. What is the main battle in the believer's heart? Galatians 5:17.
3. What is a result of being sure of salvation? II Timothy 2:19.
4. Can God keep His promise? Romans 4:21.
5. What does God give the believer? Romans 15:13.
6. Who begins and concluded our salvation? Philippians 1:6.
7. What part should Christ have in our life? Colossians 1:18.
8. How long does God's faithfulness last? I Corinthians 1:7-9.
9. Who helps us do the will of God? Hebrews 13:20-21.
10. Who can separate us from God? Romans 8:39.

*Line changed by present author.